D1193608

POLITICS POKER & PIETY

A PERSPECTIVE ON CULTURAL RELIGION IN AMERICA

wallace e. fisher

Abingdon Press

Nashville   New York

POLITICS, POKER, AND PIETY

Copyright © 1972 by Abingdon Press

ISBN 0-687-31725-8

Library of Congress Catalog Card Number: 79-175281

MANUFACTURED BY THE PARTHENON PRESS AT
NASHVILLE, TENNESSEE, UNITED STATES OF AMERICA

Dedicated to the millions of Americans who share Albert Camus' hope: "I should like to be able to love my country and still love justice."

PREFACE

The issue of church and state is an old chestnut in medieval and modern European history. More venerable yet in Christian history, it reaches back to Jesus' declaration: "Render unto Caesar . . ." Oscar Cullmann states categorically that "the question of church and state is so closely bound up with the gospel itself that they emerge together." [1]

Thus in the Cross of Christ the relationship between "Christ and Caesar" stands at once in the beginning and at the center of the Christian faith. As a corollary, the problem, "Church and State," is posed for the Church at all times, forever: "For my sake you will be dragged before princes and kings, to bear witness before them and the gentiles" (Matt. 10:18).

7

This does not mean that the Church must of necessity be persecuted by the State; it does mean, however, that it must always reckon with the fact that it *can* be persecuted by the State. The cross of Christ should lead the Church in all its deliberations about the relationship of Church and State; not just in its negative aspects, but in its positive aspects as well.[2]

But we are concerned here with more than the complex problem of church and state. Our attention will be focused on the subtle relationship between Christ and culture, faith and political action, belief and patriotism, piety and politics. The truth of these ambiguous relationships is more nearly approximated, we judge, by suggestion and description than by dogmatic statements. We are not academicians investigating ancient documents. Hugh Trevor-Roper, Regius Professor of Modern History at Oxford University, says that "historians should study the process of history and not merely the detail of the narrow sector in which they specialize." [3] We are also cognizant of Miriam Camp's admonition that "the historian should share the moods, atmosphere, and disabilities of those whose action he is reporting." [4]

Presently it is crucial that our citizenry discern something of the complex relationship between Christianity and culture, theology and political science, piety and politics, in American history. Because of the widening polarization in ecclesiastical circles and in political society over social issues (which eventually become political issues), the time is especially hospitable for this study. This book is designed for personal use by clergy, politicians, and laymen; for group study in congregations; and as collateral reading in colleges and seminaries. The extensive footnotes are guides to further reading for those who want to delve more deeply into this complex subject.

This study frames the politics-piety issue in manageable terms for serious-minded clergy, lay leaders, teachers, students, and concerned public officials. It is narrative and interpretive history. As the story unfolds, the reader will come face to face with the stark judgments of history. Hamlet remarked that the purpose of drama is "to hold as 'twere the mirror up to nature." One purpose of history certainly is to hold a mirror up to events, movements, issues, and personalities. Clergy, laity, citizens who are not members of the Christian church—and especially the young—need historical perspective on contemporary events and social issues as well as concern for persons if they expect to act responsibly in this confused period of American experience. To quote Trevor-Roper again: "We study it [history] not merely for amusement—though it can be amusing—but in order to discover how we have come to where we are." [5] The past is nonrepeatable, but our antecedents and roots are there. It is crucial that many American citizens should make that discovery, share it widely, and act responsibly in the light of it.

Intro.

Dunning Idle, Frederic Klein, and Theodore G. Tappert, professional historians, read the manuscript critically. They clarified the presentation but bear no responsibility for its content. Vincent R. Eshelman, Larry L. Lehman, and Clyde E. Brown, colleagues at the Lutheran Church of the Holy Trinity; R. Ray Evelan and Jack R. Hoffman, former colleagues at Trinity; and Harold S. Sigmar, Gabriel Fackre, Donald R. Heiges, Ruth Grigg Horting (former secretary of welfare in Pennsylvania Governor Lawrence's cabinet), Ann

Musselman, Ann Bolbach White, and Robert Moore also offered insights which improved the presentation. Mrs. Arline Fellenbaum, my secretary, prepared the manuscript. My wife, Margaret Elizabeth, and our son, Mark, a political science major at the University of North Carolina at Chapel Hill, provided understanding, support, and constructive criticism on chapters 2, 3, and 4.

Wallace E. Fisher

CONTENTS

Chapter 1

THE BREAKING STORM: POLITICS AND PIETY IN CONFLICT

A decade ago an entertaining musical, *Fiorello,* based on the life and times of Mayor LaGuardia of New York City, won critical acclaim on Broadway. The decisive dimensions of the play were its spritely music and intelligent lyrics. One of the show-stoppers—sung by a group of cigar-smoking, poker-playing, hard-drinking politicians—was titled "Politics and Poker." The musical presented an obvious reality: politics and poker have much in common. Both games depend upon a desire for power and a strategy for achieving it. They employ bluff, bold thrust, artful parry, compromise, and retrenchment.

Prodded by this observation, one recalls illustrations of it at random from American history: Clemenceau's quip that Wilson had fourteen points while the good Lord was satisfied with ten set the stage for an international "blue chip game" of diplomacy, John Kennedy's poker-skillful handling of the Cuban missile crisis, Richard Nixon's high-stakes gamble on a "Southern strategy" to win Middle-America's support. Because politics and poker have much in common, they are linked *implicitly* in this study.

"Piety" is simply there. It is a current edition of the old theme of church and state. The sentiment connoted by the word is reflective of the temper of the times. In the United States, wherever politics is, piety is never far behind and vice versa. The word piety has appeared frequently in the titles of serious articles and books since the early 1950s.[1] The times have thrust the church in many ways and places into politics, and the game has been played with and without poker-like skill, with and without political integrity. This current interaction between politics and piety threatens to rip the established churches asunder, weakening further the social fabric of American life.

The constraint to write this book on Christianity and American politics did not claim me until 1967 when the evidence that politics was polarizing the churches of America could no longer be ignored. As a parish pastor serving a culturally diverse, center-city congregation, I had experienced tensions in both church and community from preaching on social and political issues, as had my colleagues. While a cleavage had not developed in Trinity Church, my participation in eighty or so church renewal conferences throughout the nation and across denominational lines (1964-1969) convinced me that the grass-roots church is severely divided over political-social issues.[2] Jeffrey Hadden's *The Gathering Storm in the Church* documented that existential judgment.[3] Now the "storm" has broken quietly but relentlessly.[4]

The cleavage in the church is complex in origin. It is ambiguous in its manifestations. It mirrors and contributes to the deep cleavages in American society. These divisions carry the seeds of social tragedy or social betterment. Presently, however, they separate laymen from laymen, clergy from clergy, and laymen from clergy in Catholic and main-line Protestant churches and in conservative Protestant circles: Berrigan *vs.* Cooke, Thompson *vs.* Pew, Graham *vs.* McIntire.

This deepening cleavage in the church surfaced during the 1950s. It came into sharp focus in the following decade. Two Supreme Court decisions in the 1950s—one *directly* (prayer and Bible-reading in the public schools) and the other *indirectly* (equal, integrated public education)—made church people in particular and the citizenry in general freshly aware of the age-old church-state controversy. Piety and politics collided noisily and dangerously.[5] Liberal churchmen applauded the Warren Court; conservative churchmen deplored it. Some church members, supporting political rightists, called for Chief Justice Warren's impeachment and defamed liberal legislators.[6] Next the nomination and election of Catholic John Kennedy added more heat to the church-state issue. Then the civil rights struggle, the poverty campaign, the Vietnam War, campus unrest, and the ABM debate exploded the politics-piety issue into every American hamlet during the 1960s.

A Presbyterian minister, Eugene Carson Blake, now executive secretary of the World Council of Churches, was jailed in Baltimore for his part in a civil rights march (1963). A Unitarian minister, James Reeb, was clubbed to death in the "national" civil rights demonstrations in Mississippi (1963). A Baptist minister, Martin Luther King, Jr., was shot to death in Memphis (1968). David Dellinger, a middle-aged religious pacifist and Yale graduate, was one of the "Chicago Seven" (1970). A Catholic priest, Daniel Berrigan, who had been convicted for rifling selective service records in Catonsville, Maryland, and was a fugitive from the law, was captured by the FBI in August, 1970, at the Block Island home of William Stringfellow, Episcopalian lay theologian, and poet Anthony Towne, both of whom were at odds with the state.[7]

Close ties between politics and piety were underscored in the person of Billy Graham, who served as the unofficial chaplain to the Nixon administration. The late Reinhold Niebuhr and Carl McIntire, poles apart politically and theologically, attacked the "house-religion" on the Potomac. Meantime, the International Congress on Evangelism, meeting in Minneapolis in 1969, demonstrated the willingness of conservative churchmen, led by Graham's brother-in-law and co-evangelist, Leighton Ford, to relate their evangelistic efforts to social issues. Not only liberal but moderate and conservative churchmen have felt constrained to be involved in political issues. Many of their colleagues in both camps, however, have deplored and criticized their involvement.

The religious-political situation in the United States is presently ambiguous, divisive, explosive. James L. Adams, an experienced religious reporter for the *Cincinnati Post and Times-Star,* argues that church lobbying is "a story that needs telling if we are to understand the internal stresses now threat-

ening to split the church's superstructure and rip the pulpit
from the pew." [8]

There are many churchmen, lay and clerical, who are convinced that *active* involvement in politics is a vindication of
true piety.[9] Others, like Paul Ramsey, Helmut Thielicke, and
Will D. Campbell, are more cautious.[10] Professor Thielicke,
for example, argues for the liberation of the commands and
promises of God from a false restriction "to a purely personal
and private arena" and urges a shift to the church's active
recognition of God's "claim upon public life as well." He is
persuaded, however, that "the church cannot do this by advancing political and social programs. What it must do is to
show men whose consciences are bound by the Word of God
that the divine commands have particular relevance also to the
substantive decisions they make." [11]

Consequently the questions bristle: Who is right: Berrigan
or Cooke? Blake or McIntire? Bennett or Ramsey? Is Christianity secular or spiritual? Who speaks for the church? Are
churchmen competent to speak on the Vietnam War, the
ABM, poverty, race, or *any* socio-political issue? Should eccle-
siastics be a "shadow cabinet"? Is it possible for the church to
speak concretely and specifically to the world without losing
its identity? [12] On the other hand, can the church be the
church without witnessing and serving actively in the world?
Can this latter be accomplished except in specific ways in
particular places? If not, how then shall the witness be made
and the service rendered? [13]

The confusion of many laymen in addressing these questions is precipitated and compounded by substantial blocs of
clergy who are overly enthusiastic in fostering the "secular"

church or overly zealous in their advocacy of the "spiritual" church. Many laymen are offended, indeed angered, by both groups. Millions of laymen feel betrayed by the "secular" clergy, who, they judge, are destroying their inherited "Faith" which they feel they need. On the other hand, an increasing corps of "worldly" laymen feel betrayed by the "spiritual" clergy, who, they judge, are destroying biblical religion by denying its socio-political relevance. Both groups among the laity are grousing—in some places raging—because they feel the clergy ignore, despise, ridicule, and blame *them* for the current state of the church while expecting *their* financial support and neglecting *them* as human beings who also have unmet needs. Unfortunately, each group of clergy has lambasted the other publicly.[14]

Meanwhile, another bloc of clergy judge that the institutional church is finding a middle road.[15] Polarized laymen object to that stance too. It is obvious that the deep, wide cleavage among the clergy is reflected among the laity. Three distinct churches (liberal, moderate, conservative) cutting across traditional lines of demarcation could emerge during the 1970s. If the current fratricidal strife in Protestant-Catholic churches continues to escalate, it could, as the bitter modernist-fundamentalist controversy did in the 1920s, obscure and cancel the church's essential witness during the decade of the 70s.

The cleavage among the clergy in both Protestant and Catholic circles stems partially from the fact that most of them are ministering to people in a changing social situation which the clergy do not understand because its norms and values are radically different from the norms and values of the Christianity they learned in the theological schools.[16] Many do not know what to support, who to oppose, or when to do either. Some try too much; others try too little. Some are arrogant critics; others are tolerant critics. Many clergy, however, are naïve about political power, politicians, and propaganda. On the other hand, some are charged with being too knowledge-able.[17] Meantime, the majority of laymen—theologically il-literate, simplistic in political judgment, equally disoriented socially—are confused, angry, or indifferent.[18]

But the issue is more complex. Elected political representa-tives also are confused. Too few fathom the social changes which have wiped out yesterday's landmarks. Most legislators are still thinking in terms of an industrial-agrarian economy that no longer exists. Few recognize that the technological revolution has effected and is effecting radical changes in America and the world community, that what the Sovietolo-gists suggested a decade or so ago is happening—"namely that East and West would meet at some midway house, that the Soviet Union would become liberalized, the United States would adopt increasing measures of socialism."[19] The old political and cultural shibboleths simply are not valid in 1972.

But the issue is still more crucial. The church in America has never faced up to the eschatological implications of the church-state issue: an *elemental* conflict between prophetic Christianity and pragmatic politics.[20] The state—even the democratic state—relies finally on repression and coercion to accomplish its ends because it must guard its sovereignty. The church—when it is true to the gospel—relies on persua-sion, freedom, and life; and on occasion it must be at odds with any state, even the democratic state. For almost two centuries the majority in America have assumed that their national state upholds God. Witness the Civil War, in which each side claimed the support of the same God.[21] Until recently, except for a minority, American churchmen have not faced the possibility of having to choose between God and the state. The historical implications of an apocalyptic struggle over ultimate authority are to most American churchmen ambiguous, controversial, and conflictive. The church-state discussions precipitated by contemporary events (Bible reading, civil rights, Vietnam War, poverty), politicians, and churchmen, proceed presently in a no man's land where the protagonists mine each other's territory as well as their own. Yet neither church nor state in America is free of the other; they are intricately intertwined. The righteous empire is gone, but the interpenetration between pious Americanism and biblical Christianity remains.[22] The socio-political-religious situation is further complicated by the fact that some American churchmen talk and act like politicians, while some American politicians talk and behave like sawdust trail preachers—especially during election years.[23]

There is urgent need for the recognition and serious addressment of this deepening polarization over socio-political issues in our American communities. Unless these schisms are faced candidly, understood compassionately, and bridged or healed substantively, both church and state could fall apart at the seams. The suggestion that the church can opt for its youth and ignore its conservative elders is unbiblical and economically impossible. The notion that ecclesiastical statements and church mergers will overmatch the differences is naïve. The judgment that the cleavage can be healed if the church decides for or against living in the world is mechanical and unrealistic. Equally, the panaceas propounded by many politicians to heal the open wounds in our society are disabling to church, state, and society. Today, a century after Lincoln's death, few congressmen or church bureaucrats appreciate the Commoner's rugged futurism: "The dogmas of the quiet past are inadequate to the stormy present; the occasion is piled high with difficulty, and we must think anew and act anew." [24]

Disruptive social issues exist. They can be ignored, but they cannot be escaped. Because churchmen are citizens, because half the citizens are acknowledged church members, and because social issues (racism, poverty, war, ecology) become political issues, the church (Catholic-Protestant-sectarian) is "up to its steeple" in politics whether it likes it or not. As John Bennett put it more than a decade ago: "Political problems have come to be the most fateful social problems." [25] The central issue to be decided is whether the church will be part of the problem or part of the answer. Obviously, it cannot be the whole answer. A more humble expectation is dictated not only by events but also by the church's unevenly converted condition.[26] But the American democratic state does provide constitutionally for the church's responsible involvement.[27] The separation between the two institutions has never been absolutistic. Grass-roots church members are also grass-roots citizens. How the church and the state in America meet the current storm over politics and piety will determine partially the course of events and the human situation in the closing quarter of the twentieth century.

Clergy and laity, politicians and electorate must learn to accept conflict as inevitable in all areas of social and political action *and* in prophetic ministry, lay aside their self-serving charges and countercharges, inquire into political programs and brood over prophetic judgments, dialogue with one another on what it means to be human in today's world, accept gracefully the historical necessity and the biblical plea to be human, and confront current socio-political realities with integrity and courage, wisdom and compassion.[28] Samuel Lubell speaks pointedly to the current situation: "I do not think this is a time to lower our voices to whispers of distrust. This is the time to raise our voices in confidence and to demand orderly and meaningful debate on all the issues that concern us so we can reconcile at least some of our differences. Our need is not to be manipulated, but to govern ourselves." [29] Dissent from majority policies on grounds of reason and/or conscience is not only a Christian mandate but also a mark of responsible *citizenship* in the American democratic state.[30] The current socio-political situation is grave indeed when a former major league baseball pitcher, Jim Bouton, can write:

> Then there was the matter of talking too much, not to reporters, to the guys. You see, *you could* talk about the war in Vietnam, only you had to say, "Look at those crazy kids marching in the street. Why don't they take a bath?" Or you could say, "What right does Rev. Groppe have to go out in the streets like that? He should be in the pulpit where he belongs." If you said these things, no one would accuse you of talking politics, because you were right.
>
> On the other hand, if you said things like, "We've got no right to be in Vietnam," or that "Rev. Groppe is certainly making his religion relevant up there in Milwaukee," then

you shouldn't be talking about things like that, because you were wrong.[31]

James Michener observes that "if the phrase 'benign neglect' means a lowering of voices and a breathing space in which to assess what has been accomplished and what must be done next, I would obviously be in favor of it, but if it means what I think it means, I would have to oppose it. I can imagine no benefit that could come from halting our efforts for equal opportunity; I can foresee grave consequences if it is attempted." [32]

This book is written under constraint. It is my judgment that the cleavages in American society are as severe today as they were on the eve of the Civil War. We are not, I think, on the edge of widespread revolution, but there are escalating divisions and a deepening alienation among America's citizens. Disabling social fragmentation is the current threat to the American nation. It is a desperate time which holds the seeds of social tragedy or radical betterment. The freedom to decide is a dreadful responsibility on our leaders and citizenry. What is required now is not a manipulated lowering of voices but an open, candid, realistic discussion of controversial social issues. What is required is not a simple change in structures but a radical change of mind. As we approach A.D. 2001, we shall have little to celebrate—if we are still here at the dawn of a new millenium—unless we bring to these discussions on socio-political change light as well as heat, compassion as well as confrontation, humility as well as conviction. Presently, friendships are going to pieces, marriages are being strained, churchmen are shouting at one another, politicians are impugning one another's motives, and the citizenry is turning bitter over defining and achieving humane goals in our political society. The church, like society itself, is ripped by this cleavage. The "gathering storm" has broken.

* * * * *

Since we are concerned primarily in this study with American citizens, and since the citizen lives in a particular socio-political society, chapter 2 traces the emergence of the American democratic state, which has little in common with the socio-political milieu in which Jesus, Paul, Augustine, and the medieval theologians lived. Chapter 3 examines the pertinent question, "Who is the American?" Chapter 4 investigates citizen dissent and rebellion in American history and cites several overt and covert acts of the state to repress both. Chapter 5 outlines the biblical mandate for the Christian's life and witness in the world and suggests ecclesiastical stances for making that witness. Chapter 6 makes the case for political integrity in ecclesiastical circles and, by implication, Christian integrity in political circles.

Chapter 2

THE AMERICAN DEMOCRATIC STATE

The American institution [political] has been a success; so Americans think, so the reflective portion of non-American mankind must concede. But because that Constitution has been a success, it has acquired in the eyes of . . . "the People of the United States," a claim to reverence, to uncritical acceptance, that has no parallel in the world.

—D. W. Brogan

Questions of Relationships

We begin by asking what the American democratic state with its complex political machinery (checks and balances) and its ambiguous philosophy (majority rule) has in common with the totalitarian Roman state about which Jesus and Paul spoke, or the changing medieval state with which Luther, Calvin, Knox, and Cranmer dealt. Do the words of Jesus, an itinerant preacher in a despised corner of a totalitarian empire, have meaning for an American Representative, Senator, or President along the Potomac in 1972? What relationship exists between Jesus' dictum: "Render unto Caesar the things that are Caesar's and unto God the things that are God's," and the political concept, "the consent of the governed"? What is the relationship between Paul's statement in Romans 13:1:

"Let every man be subject to the powers prevailing over us," and the first ten amendments to the American Constitution which safeguard, theoretically, every individual's personal liberties against encroachment by the state?

What relationship exists between Luther's discourses to the princes, who, as rulers of the territorial state, were also "under the pulpit" as members of the church[1] and the American churches' addressment to legislators who, in a pluralistic society, are under different pulpits—Protestant, Catholic, Orthodox, Jewish, Unitarian, Mormon—or under no pulpit at all? What connection exists between the political thinking of Luther in a society where the prince determined the religion of his province, and the thinking of Jacob Javits, George McGovern, Mark Hatfield, William Fulbright, and John Stennis in a society where the state is forbidden by law to establish (or favor) a particular religion? What relation exists between the modern democratic nation-state which claims the right to preserve its sovereignty and the church which claims authority in the realm of conscience? Can any modern state, including a democratic state, honor the individual's civil liberties and religious commitments if his interpretation and exercise of those liberties and/or commitments run counter to that state's vital interests in law and order, the maintenance of which is a basic function of every sovereign state? Will a democratic state, hard-pressed, become as totalitarian as the Roman, Communist, Fascist, or Nazi states? Does the American church, enjoying constitutionally guaranteed freedom, have the right to pressure the government to adopt particular policies and/or specific programs? If the church has that right, does it effect its purpose best through political action groups, by seeking power in the political arena, or simply by persuading individual church members (citizens) to view issues from the "Christian" point of view?

These questions reflect the inevitable tension between politics and piety in America and the deepening conflict between her politicians and religionists in the closing quarter of the twentieth century. Before we can respond to these questions, we must gain some perspective on the development of the American democratic state.

Historical Background

In all societies men have found it necessary to establish certain rules of conduct to be obeyed. In primitive societies the authority for enforcement was a complex consisting of tribal elders, taboos, and social traditions. When these forces were organized institutionally, the state became a crude reality. Essentially, the elements of an effective modern state are these: (1) people, (2) a common core of belief, (3) territory, (4) government, and (5) permanence. The state emerges as a political reality when it fashions and maintains a permanent organization, occupies and controls defined territory, governs in a fashion which maintains social order, and has the means to enforce the traditions and rules which the group accepts or the state determines. When the body of rules under which the governed live are enforceable, they become laws. In civilized history the state has existed because of its institutional ability to employ force to guarantee its own sovereignty.[2] When Poland and France were unable to resist the Nazi state in 1939 and 1940, they lost their sovereignty.[3]

The most ancient states claimed gods as their founders; they rested their authority on a supernatural source (Romulus and Remus were regarded as the sons of Mars). The divine right of "Christian" kings roots in this ancient view. However, since early modern times the state has claimed that its authority rests on a social contract—a state in which the majority agree to limit their individual freedoms for the commonweal; sovereignty rests on the consent of the governed. Since the rise of the modern nation-states after A.D. 1500, a corollary theory to the consent of the governed has developed: the sovereign power of the state rests on its institutionalized military power to control and/or conquer others. This theory is inherent in Hobbes' *Leviathan,* the "politics of reality" (Realpolitik), and in the Germany of Bismarck, Wilhelm I, and Adolf Hitler. Presently, another political concept is taking shape: the state's authority rests on the cooperation which develops between diverse human groups in the natural growth of a particular society; unless it develops, government has no right to exist.[4]

As the state developed from ancient to modern times, different forms of government emerged. First, there was the tribal state. The head of the clan was owner, priest, and judge; he was lawgiver and military leader. His supremacy was unquestioned, but his status depended upon his skill to demonstrate that he represented the will of the gods. This was particularly true in the Near East, where the state in all its relationships purported to be an earthly reflection of the balance of power in heaven. The leader fixed the rights and duties of *his* people. The Jews, Greeks, and Romans appear first in history with this kind of tribal organization. The Mosaic

Code, for example, is a codification of developing legal and religious beliefs which emerged among a tribal people, characteristic of and peculiar to the world of the Middle East.[5]

A later form of government was the city-state which evolved from the agricultural village. Athens was a notable example of this form of government.[6] What the Greeks meant by "democracy" (a word they invented) was the limited measure of self-government achieved by their city-states. A degree of free discussion and individualism developed, but the basic element in the Greek idea of the democratic state was the "harmony" of life shared by the male citizens. Women, foreigners, and slaves enjoyed no civil rights. The human possibilities of the city-state are extolled in history's most significant treatise on politics, Plato's *Republic*. Its value lies in its articulation of utopian generalities. Although Plato forged the bond between individual ethics and politics, he oversimplified the socio-political problems of democracy.[7] Aristotle was more realistic; he agreed, however, that the moral idea was the main justification of the state: "the sovereignty of law, the freedom and equality of citizens, constitutional government, the perfecting of men in civilized life."[8] Aristotle appreciated that "ideals must exist not like Plato's pattern in the Heavens but as forces working in and through agencies by no means ideal."[9]

When Rome became a republic, law was separated from traditional religion and morality; it became a civil set of rules and principles designed to provide justice through rational means. This concept of Roman law has played a significant role in the development of Western civilization. It was Paul's ground for honoring civil authorities. But during the closing centuries of the empire, law was merged with the person of the emperor. Consequently, law deteriorated.

As the Empire disintegrated over three turbulent centuries, the barbarians pressed in from the north and occupied the old empire for almost five centuries. Lacking political traditions and respect for law, they responded only to force. Turmoil, lawlessness, and piracy plagued the early Middle Ages. In the ninth century Charlemagne tried but failed to establish a permanent political organization. Out of this social confusion and absence of unifying power, the system of feudalism emerged.[10]

Feudalism, a socio-political-religious society, was rooted essentially in military prowess, landholding, and *piety;* it rested on mutual responsibility (lord gave protection; vassal gave service). The supreme feudal overlord was king; his authority rested on the force he could command. It was he who granted lands to less powerful lords who became his vassals. Thus, he guaranteed their allegiance to him. Each vassal provided military service and/or customary dues for his protection. The fief was the political unit of the feudal system. Real overlordship in the Middle Ages resided as often in the religious order as in the political order, since the pope was a powerful feudal lord. The Holy Roman Empire and the papacy were in constant conflict and frequently contested bitterly over the authority to govern in this or that area of the common life. The "just price" of the Middle Ages, for example, was enforced under a religious jurisdiction. Church courts tried cases affecting property. The pope, employing the interdict, could enforce his authority and constrain a recalcitrant lord to heel by denying religious services to all the people in that lord's territory.

This was the weapon Pope Innocent III employed to force King John of England and Philip Augustus of France to acknowledge his overlordship. In 1077, Henry IV, excommunicated by the pope, knelt in the snow at Canossa for three days to be reinstated in the church. Political organization appeared to be subservient to religious authority during the Middle Ages, but Henry's restoration to grace was as much a political victory for him as for the pope. It established his power, confused his opponents, and throttled the Augsburg conclave which could have cost him his leadership. Since the German king was later able to march into Pope Gregory's territory, drive him from Rome, and set up a new pope in his place, it is evident that the religious authority gained a "victory" at Canossa only in a peripheral and pietistic sense.

During the late Middle Ages the nation-state, the primary political reality of modern times, emerged.[11] A series of wars among feudal suzerainties, like the War of Roses in medieval England, resulted in territorial consolidations. These emerging nation-states took over not only the church's political responsibilities but some of its religious rights as well. Henry VIII's quarrels with Rome were political-personal, and in Roman Catholic countries like Spain and France the states used the religious organizations for political purposes. The Spanish Inquisition contributed as much to Spain's unification as it did to maintaining religious conformity, which in itself contributed to national unity. Spanish and French colonial ventures were national forays for "the gospel, gold, and glory." The Reformation provided the opportunity for local peoples and emerging sovereignties to assert themselves against papal authority.[12] These expanding territories established governmental institutions which unified the local legislative, judicial, financial, and military operations under a single secular authority. Loyalty to the prince was the forerunner of loyalty to the nation; government was pragmatic.[13] The age of discovery and expansion also allowed the early nation-states (Holland, Portugal, Spain, England, and France) to strengthen their governmental powers; mission and mercantilism went hand in hand. The American and French revolutions in the late eighteenth century gave nationalism the appurtenances of religion: symbol (flag), hymn (national anthem), credo (pledge to the flag). A principle began to evolve that any group of people, convinced that they should be a nation, had the right to establish an independent sovereign state. In the nineteenth century the nation-states of Latin America emerged; Europe, in spite of the Treaty of Vienna, experienced a series of revolutions as the German and Italian nation-states came into existence. During those revolutionary decades, the Greeks, Poles, Slavs, and Czechs also struggled to achieve national status.[14] The principle of self-determination was finally endorsed in the Treaty of Paris at the close of World War I.

The modern nation-state has distinct marks. Each sovereign state demands absolute political independence and the right to develop as it chooses. When it judges that interests which it considers vital to its security or continued identity are threatened, it places its own needs above the interests of any individual, group, nation, or humanity itself. Each nation-state demands the right to fashion the particular form of government it chooses. Monarchy, which thrived from the sixteenth through the eighteenth centuries, disappeared during the nineteenth century in spite of efforts to maintain the political status quo after Waterloo. Oligarchy resurfaced during the twentieth century in the form of totalitarian states. A third form of government, democracy, developed rapidly in North America and western Europe during the nineteenth century. It is this form that concerns us in this study.

Viewed theoretically, a democracy is representative government by the people—or at least by a majority of the people—in the best interests of the majority with the right of dissent guaranteed to minorities. Ideally, democracy is "government of the people, by the people, for the people." [15] This particular form of government has developed steadily in America and western Europe since the late eighteenth century.

A basic motivation for political democracy resides in the rights of private property. As men gained and possessed the goods of the earth and employed them as they deemed wise, they sought to guarantee the right of individual ownership; they demanded protection for their possessions and representation in all matters of taxation.

While the concept of private property was a dynamic in the emergence of political democracy, the philosophical theory which undergirds democracy and provides popular support for it is the "social contract." [16] Man, living freely in the state of nature—so the theory goes—decided voluntarily to surrender certain of his rights to safeguard and protect other rights (life, limb, property, etc.). Since a large territorial area, well populated, could wage war and defend itself more adequately than a single feudal lord could, a number of lords agreed to make common cause. But the rights they surrendered still belonged to them; the contract was voluntary.

The Magna Carta, 1215, recognized this principle of self-determination, but only for one sixth of the population: the feudal lords. Five and a half centuries later, the Federalists in the United States were convinced that only the people of property and education were qualified to govern; they lodged that conviction in the American Constitution. Jefferson differed only in the respect that he argued to include farmers (economically poor landholders) in the election processes. Jackson enlarged the concept to include not only the small farmers but also frontiersmen and the laborers in the cities. The principle has been expanded steadily over the years until the right of woman's suffrage was granted in 1920 (Nineteenth Amendment).

In summary, these characteristics define the democratic state: a written or unwritten *constitution* which is respected, *citizenship* guaranteed and required by the state, *majority rule,* the right of *minority dissent,* the importance of *public opinion* in making and administering laws, the development of *political parties,* and adequate *material power* (force) to maintain the state's sovereignty. Every sovereign state, democratic or not, inevitably makes claims which are in conflict with egalitarian philosophy. To bring a citizen's personal freedom and personal discipline into socio-political equilibrium is a continuous, frictional, often explosive process in all political societies.

Political democracy has rivals in other forms of government which are designed to function differently. State socialism calls for a government that assumes the ownership of all major economic enterprises and the supervision of minor economic ventures in the society. The socialist state is the absolute and final adminstrator of the nation's economic system. Democratic socialism (Sweden, Finland, etc.) seeks to mitigate this absolutism through parliamentary processes and a wider participatory ethos. Communism goes all the way: it calls for the state to control *all* human activity—at least in theory. It attempts a meld of state and society. In practice, the state intimidates, coerces, and liquidates nonconformists. Anarchism, which drifts in and out of history and has currently reared its head again in America, views the state as the absolute enemy of the individual. Rejecting any need for the functions of the state, it seeks to abolish it. The anarchist argues that the individual should be supreme; the state is man's total enemy.

Since the state is an instrument for serving collective human needs, an evaluation of any particular state must be based on its determination of those needs, its ability to meet them, and the methods it employs in doing so. Under severe pressure, internal or external, the state—including the democratic state —relies on repression, coercion, and/or death to safeguard its sovereignty.[17] In seasons of extreme national crisis, the democratic state rivals the dictatorship in adopting totalitarian measures.

Against this overview of the development of the state, we turn next to sketch the evolution of the American democratic state.

The American Experiment in Democracy

Arbitrarily, we identify the beginning of the American democratic state with the Revolution of 1688 in Great Britain.

The roots of American democracy are, of course, more varied and complex. They lie deep in the Plymouth and Jamestown experiences; in the writings of Locke, Montesquieu, and Rousseau; in the Magna Carta and English common law; in the Roman republican state; in Plato's *Republic* and Aristotle's *Politics;* and in the pronouncements of the Hebrew prophets. We begin with the Revolution of 1688 because the "Bloodless Revolution" which brought William and Mary to the English throne demonstrated the supremacy of Parliament over the king even though his complete subordination to that representative assembly required another century.

George I, who, after William and Mary and Queen Anne, came to the English throne from the German state of Hanover, was not interested in British politics. He left policy-making to his ministers. When George II ascended the throne in 1727, the authority of the ministry was firmly established. George III, who became king in 1760, was the identified villain in the writings of the American colonials, but the real culprit was Parliament. In 1765 Blackstone wrote in his *Commentaries on the Laws of England:* "I know of no power which can control the Parliament." [18] But George III set out with Teutonic determination to regain what his predecessors had lost. Born in England, he "gloried in the name of Britain." [19] A skillful politician, he competed with the ministry at its own game and pressed for several of the measures which precipitated the American Revolution. But it was the Tories in Parliament who managed and lost the war against America. The three immediate effects of the War of American Independence were (1) freedom for the colonies, (2) solidification of Parliament's supremacy over the king in the evolution of English constitutional government, and (3) history's first large-scale venture in a republican form of government.[20]

The United States' initial venture in self-government was under the Articles of Confederation. The Articles, overshadowed by the Federal Constitution of 1787, provided, nonetheless, the form of government under which the new states managed to exist during the precarious decade after the American Revolution. The Annapolis Convention in 1786 and the Constitutional Convention in 1787 were convened because responsible Americans recognized the need for a federal union and a government with strong central powers. Government under the Articles had resulted in "confusion roughly organized."

Shays' Rebellion in Massachusetts in 1786, the growing competition and hostility between the sovereign states, and the worsening economic situation had persuaded the leaders in the several states that a strong federal government was essential. Washington, Hamilton, and Madison—present at the Constitutional Convention—had argued previously for a strong federal system. The convention is notable not only for who was present (Washington, Madison, Hamilton, Franklin, Gouverneur Morris, Charles Pinckney; John Adams and Thomas Jefferson, moderate radicals, were abroad at the time) but for who was absent (radicals Samuel Adams, John Hancock, and Patrick Henry).[21] The essential purpose of the convention had been defined by George Washington in 1786, when he said of the nation under the Articles of Confederation: "I do not conceive that we can exist long as a nation without having lodged somewhere a power which will pervade the whole Union in as energetic a manner as the authority of the State government extends over the several States." [22]

The Constitutional Committee worked primarily from the Articles of Confederation, adding the powers of taxation, commercial control, and coercion. Their completed work was a conservative document oriented to proprrty rights rather than to human rights. "When the Republic was founded the fathers saw no need to use the term [democracy] in the official language describing their handiwork. As the nation grew, the United States, usually then [the 1850s] a plural word, 'were' referred to as a federal system, a confederacy, or a republic, but *not* as a democracy." [23]

Employing hindsight, one can identify limitations in the Constitution. The defined power to regulate industry would have avoided turmoil after the Civil War, during the 1930s, and in the affluent 1950s and 60s, but how could men in eighteenth-century agricultural-rural America have envisioned technological-urban America? A constitutional definition of citizenship would have prevented the continuing confusion over citizenship in a state and citizenship in the United States. That discrepancy could have been resolved. Third, the powers which were *not* delegated directly to the Federal Government were reserved implicitly to the states. This created a "no man's land" which reaches from the Whiskey Rebellion of 1794 to the current appeals of George Wallace for states' rights.

Hard-fought regulating legislation partially corrected the initial weaknesses in the Constitution. The Fourteenth Amendment provided the legal corrective for the second oversight mentioned above. Meanwhile, the struggles over the interpretation of citizenship in a state and in the United

States continue; they are as significant today as they were in the days of John Marshall and Roger B. Taney.

The Constitution was not one whit more democratic than the limited suffrage granted in the states at the time the document was framed. The President and senators were not elected directly by the eligible voters. The members of the House of Representatives were elected according to the qualifications employed in the several states in voting for local legislators. But this provision automatically democratized the House as the states extended the suffrage during the nineteenth century. The direct election of senators was enacted in the early twentieth century. The issue of the electoral college remains in political limbo. The presidential election of 1968 brought it to the fore once again.

Although the Constitution was conservative, the procedure adopted for its ratification loosed revolutionary forces. The process of ratification called for conventions of delegates elected in each state by the eligible voters. It was agreed that the document would be binding on the signers as soon as nine states had ratified it.[24] Since the Philadelphia Convention had worked in secrecy, the representatives at the state conventions were largely ignorant of the contents of the Constitution. Opponents of the Constitution had little time to organize their forces; otherwise, it is likely that ratification would have failed.

Because the Constitution was the political creation of merchants, lawyers, and planters on the Atlantic seaboard, the thirteen conventions for ratification revealed the nation-wide division between the "haves" and the "have-nots." [25] The people of interior Massachusetts who had sympathized with

Shays' Rebellion, the German and Scotch-Irish of Pennsylvania, the inhabitants of the Piedmont in Virginia, and the settlers in the Carolina back country were strongly opposed to the Constitution. The wage earners in the cities would have joined these small farmers and poor plantation owners if they had been franchised voters. Even so, the anti-constitutionalists forced the Federalists to promise a series of amendments to the Constitution guaranteeing individual "rights." The first Congress under the Constitution redeemed that pledge; ten amendments, ratified, became in effect the American Bill of Rights. The First Amendment embodies the principle of separation of the institutions of church and state.

Conflicting interpretations of the Constitution, financial affairs being the specific issue, produced political parties as an elemental strand in the American governmental system.[26] Hamilton, arguing for aristocratic rule, calling for sound currency, and pressing for the establishment of a national bank, was opposed first by Madison and then by Jefferson. Mr. Jefferson, remembering his beginnings on a farm in western Virginia, became the spokesman for the farmers and the money-poor landowners. But Jefferson himself was an aristocrat; he did not trust the laboring class in the towns and cities.[27] He also argued for a strict interpretation of the Constitution in opposing Hamilton's strong fiscal policy and proposal for a national bank. The group which rallied around Hamilton were called Federalists. Those who supported Jefferson were occasionally called Democrats, more often, Republicans. Jefferson preferred the latter appellation.[28] Two parties had come into existence by the time of the second national election. The Republicans joined the Federalists in supporting

Washington, but they presented their own candidate, George Clinton, for Vice-President. Clinton ran a tight race; John Adams was elected by a seventy to fifty vote in the electoral college. At the third national election the Republicans won, placing Jefferson in the White House.

The War of 1812 was a second American Revolution waged for economic and cultural independence. It was a frontiersmen's war. Fostered by the West (the War Hawks), it was bitterly opposed by the people of New England. In fact, it precipitated the Hartford Convention (Connecticut) of 1814 which brought together representatives of New England to consider not only the defense of their area against the British (who then occupied the Maine coast) but also secession from the Federal Union. The treaty of peace and Jackson's victory over British troops at New Orleans halted whatever plans for secession the New Englanders may have entertained.[29] By 1816 the Federal party was dead. One New Englander observed that the Republicans had become so nationalistic that they had "out federalized Federalism."[30] The National Republican and the Democratic parties took shape during the 1820s. With John Quincy Adams' defeat by an electoral vote of 178-83, a new breed of politician—"the Jacksonian democrat"—signalized the triumph of the people.[31]

The Virginia dynasty—Jefferson, Madison, Monroe—had governed the young nation until 1824. John Quincy Adams had been narrowly elected president in 1824. Expectedly, therefore, the election of 1828 turned into a democratic "revolt" which swept Andrew Jackson into the White House. The first "common man" to occupy the presidency was a hard-nosed Unionist but a thorough-going western democrat in every other respect. Jackson blocked the rechartering of the national bank, slowed down the building of national roads, contributed to the democratization of the American political system, and introduced the spoils system.[32] Without intending to do so, he fostered sectionalism.

From the beginning, sectionalism was a disrupting force in the young nation—first between the tidewater and the back-country and then among the South, West, and Northeast. The first serious breach was precipitated by South Carolina's effort to defy federal law in 1830.[33] Jackson responded by threatening to use federal troops to enforce the law. That was the year Jackson and one of his Cabinet members, the influential southern statesman John C. Calhoun, parted political company. The break was dramatized, and America's next thirty years were cleanly defined, by the toasts which were made at Jackson's birthday dinner on April 13, 1830. Jackson declared firmly, "Our federal Union; it must be preserved!" Calhoun proposed, "The Union; next to our liberty most dear! May we all remember that it can only be preserved by respecting the rights of the states." [34] Men like Calhoun, Clay, and Webster, pursuing different purposes, united in spite of their differences to engineer two major compromises (1830 and 1850) which in effect allowed the North time to establish the lineaments of union with the western states and the border states before the deep South seceded in the winter of 1860-61. A civil war in the United States prior to 1860 could have ended differently.

During the quarter century between Jackson and Lincoln the young American nation engaged in the Mexican War. It was the third war in seven decades for bumptious, nationalistic, violence-oriented America. Expansionism, ebullience, slavery, and chauvinism precipitated the war. President Polk, acting much as President Lyndon Johnson later acted on the Tonkin Gulf Resolution, announced that the Mexicans in a border raid had spilled blood on American soil and called for war. Lincoln, then in the House, asked to see the "spot," but Congress authorized men and money for the imperialistic venture. Immediately, Polk announced to his Cabinet: "In making peace with our adversary, we shall acquire California, New Mexico, and other further territory, as an indemnity for this war, if we can." [35] In that single sentence, President Polk provided his contemporaries and history with the reason for the war: national expansion. It was a season when the majority of Americans were convinced that they should have all of Mexico and Canada as well. They considered that it was their manifest destiny to occupy North America.[36]

Meanwhile, the Whig party had replaced the National Republicans, but after a brief flurry it also died. The present-day Republican party, formed in opposition to slavery, was born at Ripon, Wisconsin, in 1854. Boldly conceived, it was a confrontational party endorsing "free land, free men, and Fremont." Its first foray on the national level, 1856, was strong enough to define the sectional struggle and the four-way presidential contest of 1860.[37] The Republicans in the North supported the Union and opposed the extension of slavery. The Democrats, now divided North and South, supported Stephen Douglas in a middle course. The Constitutionalists (Southerners committed to "federalism") named John C. Bell as their candidate. The Southern radicals (secessionists) named John C. Breckinridge as their standard-bearer.[38]

Abraham Lincoln was elected as a minority President. The South had served notice that his election would mean secession and, if necessary, war. They acted on both threats. Roy Nichols has commented on the South's decision to fight: "At certain times and in certain circumstances, cooperative behavior predominates; but competitive behavior is seldom if ever absent, and when too vigorously aroused, leads to a strife which ranges from argument to war." [39] Both North and South expected early victory. The military competence of the Confederate officers brought the South within a shade of achieving their goal in the first two years.[40] But technology, as well as numbers, was on the side of the North. The sewing machine guaranteed an adequate supply of uniforms and shoes. The reaper freed rural men for military service and provided bread for the armies. The railroads and telegraph lines, which had expanded rapidly after 1850, facilitated troop movements and helped to bind the North and West together.[41]

At the outset of the Civil War, Lincoln had assured the South that the preservation of the Union, not the abolition of slavery, was the Union's military objective. But a substantial bloc of Northerners saw it otherwise. Responding to Horace Greeley's urgent demand for abolition, Lincoln wrote on August 22, 1862: "My paramount object in this struggle is to save the Union. . . . If I could save the Union without saving any slave, I would do it; and if I could save it by freeing all the slaves, I would do it; and if I could save it by freeing some and leaving others alone, I would also do that."

Lincoln's personal views on slavery had been enunciated in the 1858 debate with Stephen Douglas; he opposed it vigorously. But as President of a nation divided by active rebellion and split irreconcilably in the North over the purpose of the War, Lincoln's primary aim was the preservation of the Union. Nonetheless, popular feeling eventually forced him to free the slaves. Following the stand-off battle at Antietam in September, 1862, President Lincoln issued the Emancipation Proclamation, effective January 1, 1863, in those states still in rebellion.[42] The Thirteenth Amendment, ratified in 1865, ended slavery in all the states and territories of the Union. But two and one-half centuries of slavery had been embedded in American history. The consequences of that inhumanity to man (racism, protest, pillage, rape, riot) continue to wound the American psyche and disrupt American society.[43]

The divisions in the North were not healed by Lincoln's proclamation. It is unlikely that he would have been reelected in the 1864 campaign against Democrat George B. McClellan if it had not been for the successes of his generals in the field— Sherman, Sheridan, and Grant.[44] In 1865 Lincoln almost despaired of binding up the nation's wounds; his inaugural address was as much a theological document as a political document. Whether he could stem the tides of hate and despair which were rampant in the nation ceased to be an option in American history when Mr. Lincoln was assassinated at Ford's Theater on April 14, 1865. The war on the battlefields was over, but the strife did not end there. Decades later, Bruce Catton wrote realistically about the war in the final volume in a centennial history of the Civil War: "Something had been won; but it was nothing more, and at the same time nothing less, than a chance to make a new approach toward a goal that had to be reached if the war and the nation that had endured it had final meaning. The ship was moving through Lincoln's dream toward a dark indefinite shore; it had a long way to go and the sky contained no stars the ordinary mortal could see. All that was certain was that the voyage was under way." [45]

Until the disputed election of 1876, the discredited Democratic party was castigated as the party of rebellion. As immigrants—especially the Irish—poured into America after the Civil War, the party was viewed as the representative of "rum, Romanism, and rebellion." The Republican party, forsaking its initial concern for free men and free land, became essentially the party of business and industry—the political instrument of people of property and position. Although Republican dominance was challenged steadily from 1876 until 1932, the Democratic party captured the White House only four times—twice under Grover Cleveland and twice under Woodrow Wilson. Even so, Cleveland was strong on property rights and Wilson was a minority President, elected in 1912 because Theodore Roosevelt had split the Republican party, and narrowly reelected in 1916 because "he kept us out of war." The efforts of the Democrats to elect a Catholic liberal candidate in 1928 ended in disaster for the party; the "solid South" bolted for the first time since the Civil War.

During the depression and World War II, the Democrats held the presidency for twenty years under Franklin Delano Roosevelt and Harry S. Truman. At mid-century, the Republican party was judged dead as a national party by many, but certain of its key figures, Henry Cabot Lodge among them, prevailed on the unprecedentedly popular General Dwight D. Eisenhower to seek the nomination for the presidency.[46] A bitter fight ensued in the Republican party between the Taft supporters and the Eisenhower enthusiasts. Universally popular, General Eisenhower, nominated in 1952 and renominated in 1956, overwhelmed urbane, witty, socially sensitive, politically cosmopolitan Adlai Stevenson in both elections.[47]

In 1960 John Fitzgerald Kennedy, an Irish Catholic Democratic senator, was elected President by the narrowest of margins. This time technology shaped politics directly. Critical observers agree that the Kennedy-Nixon television debates transformed the little-known, untested, youthful Senator Kennedy into a President. This nationalization of presidential politics continues to be a consequence of television's nationalization of the voter audience. By 1970 senatorial elections had been nationalized too.

President Kennedy's assassination in Dallas, Texas, on November 22, 1963, elevated Lyndon B. Johnson to the presidency. In 1964 the conservative wing of the Republican party bulldozed the Republican National Convention and nominated Arizona Senator Barry Goldwater, whose thinking echoed the nineteenth century so plainly that Mr. Johnson was elected in a landslide vote which rivaled the vote Franklin Roosevelt received in 1936. But Johnson's consensus politics failed to unite a rapidly fragmenting America. The widening negative reaction to the President's leadership persuaded him to step down. Many Americans, and especially Democrats, felt betrayed by Johnson's escalation of the war in Vietnam. They remembered how he had declared in Akron, Ohio, on October 21, 1964, "We are not about to send American boys

47

nine or ten thousand miles away from home to do what Asian boys ought to be doing for themselves." [48] The election of 1968 placed Richard M. Nixon in the nation's executive office as a minority President. The strife-ridden Democratic party faltered. George Wallace's strength as the "conservative" candidate threatened to throw the election into the House. The 1970 mid-term elections demonstrated the revived strength of the Democratic party as it swept more than a dozen governors' offices and maintained its control of Congress. The party, fragmented by the disastrous Chicago Convention and riot, girded its loins for the presidential battle of 1972.

* * * * *

In the course of American history, the democratic state has enacted and the people have ratified sixteen constitutional amendments to the original ten, including a legal guarantee on the citizenship of blacks, the provision for the direct election of senators, the establishment of a graduated income tax, the right of woman suffrage, prohibition (repealed in 1933), and the legal limitation of two terms for the presidency. The state has been imaginative and realistic enough, and its written Constitution has been flexible enough, to enable the government to accommodate to the drastic social, economic, and cultural changes which transformed the rural-agricultural society of eighteenth-century America into the urban-industrial society of the twentieth century.

During the nation's turbulent history, the American democratic state had transformed itself from sovereign states in rebellion (1775-1783) into a political entity (1789-1830). It had maintained the Union first by compromise and then by military force (1830-1865). It had abolished the social institution of slavery (1865). It had adapted to the rapid socio-economic changes after the Civil War by a massive program of regulation of private interests (1870-1920). It had coped imaginatively with America's stake in a worldwide economic depression (1930-1940). It had helped to check nazism and fascism and emerged as one of the two semi-continental world powers (1940-1945). It had rallied the "free" world to hold its own against Soviet communism in a grim "cold war" (1948-1960). But could it cope—in concert with other social institutions— with the widening cultural revolution that raged across the world?

The American democratic state experienced deep internal changes in its political traditions in the course of its two-hundred-year history. From the initial compromise in the Constitutional Convention on how the states should be represented (the small states feared a democracy of numbers), American politics moved steadily toward making the government a system of majority rule.[49] In principle this thorny issue was an elemental cause of the Civil War. John C. Calhoun had insisted that the Founding Fathers had not planned to set up "a democracy of numbers," but had intended instead that the legislators should represent broad economic interests. The Civil War was the tragic cost of settling that issue by force in favor of a democracy of numbers; the majority compelled the minority to accept its dictum. When the Supreme Court decreed recently that congressional districts should be reapportioned, it took another step in America's continuing efforts to make its politics responsive to majority rule. "Legislators represent people, not trees or acres," Chief Justice Warren declared in 1964. "Legislators are elected by voters, not farms or cities or economic interests." [50] This change would please a Jefferson, a Jackson, or a Lincoln, because it extends democracy. But will democracy work in an automated, technological society of numbers? Does the nation need, as Rex Tugwell and others argue, a new Constitution? Or can the government, which has changed substantially since its founding, interpret and amend its Constitution so that it can adapt to current social needs?

Is American Democracy Viable?

During the 1960s the American democratic state found itself embattled from within and without. It entered into a technological race with Russia to reach the moon, a contest with military significance despite denials by both sides. It became ambiguously embroiled in Vietnam's war for national liberation. It faced a generation of youth in rebellion. It wrestled ineffectively with the revolutionary demands of 20,000,000 blacks and 30,000,000 poverty-ridden whites. It experienced rejection in Latin America and Asia for its "dollar diplomacy." It suffered unpopularity in western Europe for its "imperialist" war in Southeast Asia.

At a deeper level, the American institution of government experienced a revolution in the American political consciousness. This significant revolution was "accomplished not by laws or constitutional amendments but by all the forces shaping American life—by our economy, our technology, our systems of education, and our new modes of scientific thought. It had begun by the early years of this century, but reached a clamorous climax in our time. It has transformed the very meaning of political numbers, has given new content to the very notions of majority and minority. It has even undermined the very assumptions on which the system of majority rule traditionally had rested." [51]

In America's representative form of government a mystique attaches itself to the secret ballot. Daniel Boorstin calls this "the sacrament of the ballot box." In the voting booth the silent voice of the people is expressed; the voice of the majority may be mistaken for the voice of God. Whose voices are speaking? What are they really saying? When do they constitute a political mandate? Bill Moyers, traveling across America in 1970 and listening to scores of individual Americans, observed that "there were thirty-five million more of us [than a decade previously]; we seemed more raucous than ever, and no one could any longer be sure who spoke for whom." [52]

The mystery surrounding the *secret* ballot was not bequeathed by the Founding Fathers. Kentucky enacted the first secret-ballot law on February 24, 1888.[53] Previously, voters had stood up among their neighbors to express their preference, which was marked on a public board. Next, parties printed their tickets in different colors, but one could see the color of his neighbor's ticket if he cared to. Reformers pressing for the Australian (secret) ballot argued that it would prevent intimidation and bribery, thus clarifying the voice of the majority.[54]

Presently, the mystery of the secret majority has been dispelled by public opinion polls, which originated in a sociology that argued that society can study itself. A concerned Walter

Lippmann was examining the significance of polled public opinion as far back as 1922. If public opinion could be polled accurately—and it had become almost a science by 1972—it could also be catered to and manipulated. TV provided the perfect medium for that. By 1968 it was possible to package and sell candidates like soap, perfume, and shaving lotion.[55] By 1970 the costs of that packaging were becoming prohibitive for congressional candidates unless they were wealthy or could corral several millions of dollars from interested contributors. It had also become questionable whether the *secret* majority spoke for the status quo, God, or the devil—or if it existed at all. Socially estranged minorities were convinced that it spoke diabolically. Others, comfortably situated, identified the majority voice with the voice of God. Education and technology had created a manipulable political consciousness which a Jefferson, a Jackson, or a Lincoln could not approve.

If the 1890s were the watershed which divided rural-agricultural America from urban-industrial America, World War II and the subsequent quarter century constituted another watershed which divided urban-industrial America from urban-suburban-technological America. During the 1960s this rampaging technology threatened to inundate the nation's sluggish social, political, economic, and religious institutions; jets, missiles, computers, automation, and moon-landings transformed society so rapidly that the social and political institutions which were creakingly effective in the 1930s and 40s appeared to be antiquated in the 1960s. By 1970 Massachusetts Institute of Technology's Marvin Minsky was arguing that the machine, which had dehumanized man, could "rehumanize" him. Professor Minsky predicted "that during the

1970s (perhaps as soon as three years) a machine will be developed with the general intelligence of an average human being.... But it is the self-improvement of the machine which will prove most astonishing: by educating itself, the machine will attain genius level in just a few months." [56] Other computer creations have been programmed for "love," "fear," and "anger."

Alan Geyer, *Christian Century* editor, pointed out some sobering social issues spawned by the machine.

> Herbert Simon of Carnegie-Mellon University has warned that the rapid automating of most routine labor operations could cause the Puritan work ethic to collapse too quickly, leaving millions to succumb to the "diseases of leisure." Already the heavy dependence of government, the military, the economy, the postal service, education and medicine upon computers has raised new risks of political manipulation, repression and depersonalization. Given the expectation that computers themselves will soon be able to reproduce prodigious offspring far more intelligent and complex than their parents, where will it all end? Even Minsky admits: "Once the computer got control, we might never get it back. If we're lucky, they might decide to keep us as pets." [57]

The last quarter of the twentieth century will record whether the democratic forms of government which had served the nation adequately from 1789 to 1960 will prove useful in a society fragmented by a cultural revolution or whether wholly new forms must be devised. By 1972 the government had responded through its traditional democratic processes to some of the pressures produced by that revolution: increasing "withdrawal" from the Vietnam war, civil rights legislation, public housing legislation, poverty programs, nuclear treaties, uneasy negotiation with Communist states, peripheral ecological reforms, fumbling efforts to revise the welfare system, and eclectic plans for an economy of peace. But the nation was divided. No one had brought it together. A substantial segment of society insisted loudly that the pace of political change was too slow. Another segment argued stubbornly that the pace was too rapid. Meantime, the cultural revolution spread and deepened. Time, some feared, was running out. Would the American democratic state find in its Constitution, its politicians, and its people's political consciousness a continuing *raison d'être?* James Michener, writing on the quality of American life in 1970, philosophized:

> In the years during which I worked in Japan, a nation crushed by defeat, I frequently suspected that because Japan was a homogeneous unit, with well-defined national goals and identifications, she stood a good chance of maintaining her existence indefinitely, pretty much as she then was. . . . I have never felt that assurance about the United States, for we are a volatile nation, subjected to divisive forces in religion, national origins and race. Our very brilliance is our enemy, our success our point of weakness. If we make a series of wrong decisions, we could very well become a group of fragmented units while less fortunate but more compact nations cope successfully with lesser problems. I have said that I believe our nation will be in strong existence two and even three hundred years from now, but I base that hope upon my trust in the American people to make certain right decisions.[58]

In this context Daniel Boorstin has written an insightful essay entitled "The New Barbarians." [59] He argues that America has moved from *experience* (an appeal to what we share) to *sensation* (an appeal to what is inexpressible). That appears to be a substantially accurate evaluation. Existentialism is in the saddle. Millions of Americans rush from instant sex to instant success to instant peace with little concern for reason, objectivity, or tradition, and with little sense of the tragedy of life or the ambiguities of history.[60] These rootless, disillusioned people, Boorstin judges, are not *egalitarians* (like those who impressed Tocqueville and Bryce) but *egolitarians*. They do not seek meaning for society as the true radicals (interested in root issues) did; they seek power for themselves. Boorstin states it baldly: "The appeal to violence and 'direct action' as if they were ends rather than means is eloquent testimony of the New Barbarians' lack of subject matter." [61]

There is descriptive truth in Boorstin's analysis, but his conclusion is too pat to explain the rebellion of blacks, poor people, and youth. When legitimate student critiques at Columbia University gathered dust in President Grayson Kirk's files for seven months before the student uprising, who is to blame for the debacle there? [62] When President Nixon deliberately remained indoors and watched television while 500,000 peace protestors descended on Washington, D. C., in the autumn of 1969, who is to blame for student unrest the following spring and the efforts to stall the Federal Government in May, 1971? When young people, who have the primary stake in the Vietnam war, recoiled angrily from the arbitrary foray into Cambodia, who is to blame for Kent

State, Jackson State, etc.? When blacks riot in Watts, Camden, and Detroit because they are jobless and live in overcrowded, rat-infested, rent-gouging tenements, who is to blame? When the poor encamp at Washington because they lack the skills to compete in a technological society, who is to blame? When American Indians and migrant workers in the California vineyards agitate for decent living standards and the opportunity to be human beings, who is to blame? [63]

Concerning the deep-seated alienation of so many youth from contemporary society, Michael Novak has written:

> *Easy Rider* is utterly powerful. And like *Bonnie and Clyde,* it is the sight and feel of blood—but their own—that makes the present five-year crop of young people sit in horror, silence, and hatred. Life is unfair. . . . To kill or to be killed, those seem to be the limits of life. Lieutenant Calley at My Lai is the unattractive surrogate for a generation. Pump bullets into others in rage: was Calley killing General Hershey when, allegedly, he pumped automatic fire into Oriental human beings? Was he tearing apart the body of J. Edgar Hoover, or Lyndon Baines Johnson, or Richard Nixon, or John Kennedy, or Martin Luther King? There seems to be enough rage to drown us all in blood, randomly, senselessly, like Clyde pulling the trigger in the surprised face of the banker. . . . Tormented souls will not be satisfied with administrative schemes.[64]

Our American social institutions are adapting to the massive, urgent human demands set in motion by the technological-cultural revolution of the last hundred years, but they are adapting too slowly and too mechanically. Until the leaders and participants in our socio-political institutions identify basic causes of human frustration and alienation, set out seriously to correct them, and unify the new minorities through common goals, American society will be disrupted by dissent, abusive rhetoric, violence, and "copping out." Presently, our social institutions—inadequately responsive to the current cultural revolution (politics, economics, social relations and concepts, religious relations and concepts)—spawn and nurture the "egolitarians." Simultaneously, Middle America recoils from and isolates these abrasive radicals; it appears to feel too threatened and disheartened to try to understand dissent as abusive as the students' "Up against the wall, you. . . !" and the blacks' impassioned "We shall have our manhood. We shall have it, or the earth will be leveled by our attempts to gain it." [65] Middle America is slow to identify and wrestle with the causes of social discontent. (George III, Lord Townsend, and Lord North did not probe the socio-economic issues which provided a platform for Samuel Adams, Thomas Paine, and Patrick Henry. They responded simplistically with repression. Consequently, they lost the colonies.) Too many comfortable Americans, grown fat on their freedom, seek currently to limit the freedom of others less comfortable than they. Both church and state bury their differences to condemn those whom they brand as religious and political heretics. Rosemary Haughton, Catholic lay writer, has defined this tragic reality.

They [church and state] speak in the name of the decencies of life, of the need for order and obedience and continuity and loyalty and tradition. They ask for consideration for ordinary people, who want to live in peace and bring up their families and try to do good and avoid evil. They know that people need the support of external norms, the sense of concrete achievement, the security of enduring structures and the sense of belonging. They encourage (at least in theory) the cultivation of virtue, the practice of charity and justice and self-denial. They fear, because it upsets people, whatever is violently different, unregulated, or spontaneous, though they will put up with it as long as it confines itself to areas of living that they consider unimportant. The Church can tolerate eccentricity that confines itself to oddities of opinion among intellectuals in small discussion groups, whose words carry little weight. . . . In the same way the state will put up (not too gracefully) with anti-nuclear demonstrations in England, because they are ineffective. Demonstrations against the Vietnam War in America roused official wrath and punishment because they struck effectively at the notion that the government in power really is a sufficient expression of the reality of the whole people. To the state, a particular war which it has undertaken is its proper work, and at once becomes so essential to its being that to question its worthwhileness is to challenge the state's very existence.[66]

The tangled task of responding politically and religiously to social change in America is complicated by suspicion, fear, anger, and galloping cultural change. It is also complicated by a religion which legitimatizes the status quo. It is complicated further by the welter of subcultures in which Americans live.

While the United States is the beneficiary of and contributor to Western culture, it is markedly different from homogeneous

English, French, or German culture. In the United States the residents of New York City differ culturally from their fellow citizens in Biloxi, Mississippi. The subculture in southern California is strikingly different from the subculture in Indiana. Some main-line Philadelphians are more comfortable in Kensington, London, than in Los Angeles; some New Yorkers prefer Paris and Rome to Seattle and Dallas. These differences in subcultures have a decided influence on both politics and piety throughout the United States. During the nineteenth century the collision course between subcultures which embraced conflicting economic goals, social purposes, and political ideologies ended violently in America's Civil War. The churches, like the political parties, promptly divided—North and South.

In every decade in American history subcultural tensions have seethed behind the facade of national "unity." On occasion these tensions have broken into the open (the Whiskey Rebellion, the New England Confederation, South Carolina's Nullification Acts, the Civil War, the protests of farmers, laborers, blacks, youth, etc.). The political aspect of this continuing conflict came into plain view when George Wallace won the presidential electors of Georgia, Alabama, Mississippi, Louisiana, and Arkansas; captured substantial segments of the political constituencies of Florida, South Carolina, North Carolina, Tennessee, Kentucky, and Virginia; and made serious inroads in a number of northern cities in the national election of 1968. Wallace's 1970 election to the governorship in Alabama demonstrates the vitality of sectionalism in 1972. The efforts in the late 1960s and early 70s to rebuild the Republican party by capitalizing on these subcultural (sectional) differences in American society have been divisive, as they were in 1856 and 1860.[67]

But it is equally essential to bear in mind that the forces which hold America together are also complex, vigorous, and deep-rooted. It is historically unrealistic and politically naïve to ignore this salutary cultural reality.

We have traced the growth of majority rule in the United States from its roots in the Constitution's social contract concept (consent of the governed) to the "one man–one vote" ruling of 1964. The rule of the majority provides for the orderly pursuit of national goals and policies, but it also bears the seeds for a tyranny of the many over minorities. We have also identified sectional differences, social and political cleavages, and cultural diversities in the history of the American nation. Cultural diversity provides a check to the threat of dictatorial federalism; but, polarized, it threatens presently to tear the nation asunder.

Before we can respond to the questions posed at the beginning of this chapter, we must first get an impression of the American and then examine specific strands of dissent and rebellion in his political and religious experience.

Chapter 3

THE AMERICAN

What then is the American, this new man?
—Crevecoeur

Prior to World War II Leslie Howard, the late international
motion picture star, played the leading role in a film titled
The Scarlet Pimpernel. In it Mr. Howard portrayed a complex
character—Robin Hood, Sherlock Holmes, and D'Artagnan
rolled into one; he was the Scarlet Pimpernel, righting wrongs
and punishing evildoers. The Scarlet Pimpernel was haunting-
ly elusive.

> They seek him here,
> They seek him there,
> They seek him everywhere,
> The Scarlet Pimpernel.

That is also true of the American. His image is changing,
elusive, never fixed long enough for anyone to say precisely

who he really is. Is he rational or irrational? Christian or pagan? Spiritual or secular? Politic or impolitic? Fair-minded or prejudiced? Affectionate or mean? Violent or conciliatory? Who is the American?

On the one hand, the American's image is ugly. It is a matter of grim record that he uses power for his own purposes, burns his cities, pollutes his air, ravages his own and others' countrysides, and practices genocide (the Indian campaigns and Vietnam). On the other hand, the American's image is magnificent. He takes heroic positions, acts out his honest concern for others, shares generously, and lays down his life for his friends and his principles.

The American's image is mixed. The American criticizes his young savagely, yet he educates and tends to worship them. He invents and uses atomic and napalm bombs while working simultaneously for a stable international order. He exploits the earth's resources while suing Chevron Oil Company for a massive oil spillage in the Gulf of Mexico. The American's image is complex. He is an enigma. Nonetheless, certain lineaments in his image can be identified.

The Revolutionary Strain in the American

Whatever else the American is, he is a man with revolution in his blood. Lord Acton, reviewing James Bryce's *American Commonwealth,* wrote in 1889:

> The story of the revolted colonies impresses us first and most distinctly as the supreme manifestation of the law of resistance, as the abstract revolution in its purest and most

perfect shape. No people was so free as the insurgents; no government less oppressive than the government which they overthrew. Those who deem Washington and Hamilton honest can apply the terms to few European statesmen. Their example presents a thorn, not a cushion, and threatens all existing political forms, with the doubtful exception of the federal constitution of 1787. It teaches that men ought to be in arms even against a remote and constructive danger to their freedom. . . . Here or nowhere we have the broken chain, the rejected past, precedent and statute superseded by unwritten law, sons wiser than their fathers, ideas rooted in the future, reason cutting as clean as Atropos.[1]

Dissent is characteristic of the American; violence is a strand in his life-style. In fact "violence has been a fundamental and grim characteristic of the American past."[2] Violence has been used often and quite purposefully; "a full reckoning with that reality is an essential ingredient in any national self-image."[3] John Smith created a police state at Jamestown. A bloc of passengers on the *Mayflower* threatened revolt before disembarkation at Plymouth Rock. A full-scale rebellion broke out in 1676 in colonial Virginia when Nathaniel Bacon led his embittered frontiersmen against the landowners in that Crown colony. The United States government was less than a half decade old when it was forced to move in military strength against the recalcitrant Scotch-Irish frontiersmen of western Pennsylvania (Whiskey Rebellion). In the nineteenth century, America, like Russia and China in the twentieth century, suffered a bloodbath (Civil War) to establish her sovereign state. The nation has a long history of violence between the races, capital and labor, and ethnic groups. Although that violence has been more often *repressive* (the tyranny of the majority which Tocqueville dreaded in his classic study of America in the 1830s) than *revolutionary,* it has been violence nonetheless.

Lord Acton observed correctly that the American was conceived in an act of revolutionary violence which claimed natural law for its authority. In chapter 2 we noted that violence, with and without sanction, has persisted in American life: the Whiskey Rebellion, New England's plans for secession, South Carolina's proposed rebellion, etc. Throughout the 1850s secession was the chief topic of conversation in the South, and by the end of 1861 eleven southern states had translated their seditious threats into devastating action. Both Lincoln and Davis invoked the Constitution to support their section's armed violence—one to suppress rebellion, the other to carry on rebellion.[4] Americans have scarcely begun to understand their own Civil War as a massive event in purposive violence in which each party believed its cause to be righteous.[5] The American Civil War was, in part, a "religious" war.[6]

Since the colonial beginnings in the early seventeenth century, violence has been employed frequently to achieve economic, ethnic, and national ends in America. Most citizens and churchmen recoil from Rap Brown's statement: "Violence is as American as apple pie." But violence is a firm strand in the national character of the American. Why is this true? Historian Michael Wallace replies:

> Two answers seem important here: first, Americans have accepted the Horatio Alger myth, never doubting that ours was a society in which all groups had the opportunity to

advance and prosper peacefully. For a variety of reasons—abundance of resources, a frontier safety valve, absence of feudal institutions or class divisions, the two-party system—ours was an open, fluid system. Second, with the exception of the Civil War and Reconstruction, only a tiny fraction of our violence has been directed against the state. Perhaps because we have been conditioned by the European experience to consider only anti-state violence truly significant, we have been prone to dismiss the American varieties.

But if we shift our focus on violence and look at its place in relations between groups rather than in relation to the state, violence assumes a much larger significance in our history. . . . Americans have often eschewed the normal electoral processes and have taken their quarrels into the streets. . . . The great bulk of our violence, at least until the 1960s, has been *repressive* rather than expressive or insurrectionary.[7]

The American has violence in his blood; he was conceived, born, and nurtured in strife. But *that* does not wholly explain him. By birth or heritage he is a European, African, Asiatic, North American Indian, or Latin American whose person was shaped by the economic opportunities, space, natural resources, and national security provided by continental North America. The American was influenced by adventure, idealism, religion, space, pluralism, and technology, as well as by violence. We shall explore these influences further.

The Buoyant American

Insight is gained into the American's life-style (his character in the context of an emerging American culture) if we listen critically to perceptive evaluators who, between 1782 and 1970, have wrestled with the question, "Who is the American?"

The first to ask the question, "Who is the American?" after the British surrender at Yorktown in 1781 was a Frenchman who, having fought alongside the Colonials in the American Revolution, settled in America. Staking out a farm in western New York, Hector St. John de Crevecoeur asked, "What then is the American, this new man?" Crevecoeur's perspicacious *Letters from an American Farmer* was first published in 1782, a year before the Treaty of Paris formally concluded the American Revolution. He answered his question in this fashion:

> He is either an European, or the descendant of an European . . . who, leaving behind him all his ancient prejudices and manners, receives new ones from the new mode of life he has embraced, the new government he obeys, and the new rank he holds. . . . I could point out to you a man whose grandfather was an Englishman, whose wife was Dutch, whose son married a French woman, and whose present four sons have now four wives of different nations. . . . Individuals of all nations are melted into a new race of men.[8]

The American was a new man, as Crevecoeur saw him, because of his new government, new station of equality, new opportunity, new land, and new blood. The American was an immigrant, like Crevecoeur, or a descendant of immigrants, living in a spacious new world where land was plentiful and opportunity expansive. The settlement of America was not, like the Norman Conquest or the Spanish Conquest of Central and South America, a clash of conquerors and native population which ended in amalgamation. It was instead "the clash of many well-defined, transplanted European cultural and religious groups—English Roman Catholic, Anglicans, Presbyterians, Congregationalists, Baptists, and Quakers; of German Lutherans, Reformed, and the 'sectaries,' and a host of others." [9] These Europeans robbed the unassimilated Indians of their humanity and imported Africans as slaves; they did not intermarry with either race.

Fifty years later another Frenchman, Alexis de Tocqueville, was struck by the "egalitarian" character of American life east of the Mississippi: "Among the novel objects that attracted my attention during my stay in the United States, nothing struck me more forcibly than the general equality of conditions." [10] In 1831 Tocqueville, touring America with his compatriot Beaumont, wrote: "The whole society seems to have melted into a middle class. . . . All the Americans whom we have encountered up to now . . . seem to have received, or wish to have received, a good education. . . . All the customs of life show this mingling of the two classes which in Europe take so much trouble to keep apart." [11] But he was describing only *white North Europeans* who had been in America for generations or who had recently arrived. In Tocqueville's America of 1831 the nonwhite was already "the invisible man."

Tocqueville was persuaded that the American's love of equality and devotion to liberty were rooted in his commitment to Christianity: "There is no country in the whole

world in which the Christian religion retains a greater influence over the souls of men than in America, and there
can be no greater proof of its utility, and of its conformity to
human nature, than that its influence is most powerfully
felt over the most enlightened and free nations on earth." [12]
But the American's religion did not motivate him to treat
blacks and Indians as persons. Nat Turner's rebellion occurred
in the same year that Tocqueville was writing glowingly
about American egalitarianism. During the decade of the
1830s the government was also engaged in the Black Hawk
Indian wars which forced more aborigines to flee farther west
or accept life on reservations. Neither church nor state viewed
the blacks or reds as human beings. Tocqueville's American
was (a) a "new" man (heredity and environment), (b) a
white egalitarian, (c) a "religious" man (conventional).

Henry Steele Commager, writing twelve decades later,
judged that America at the opening of the twentieth century
was a "Christian" nation in all respects except law. Christianity
was recognized in some states as the official but not the established religion. Jurors were required to believe in God, teachers to read from the Bible, and in some states a religious ob-
servance of the "Lord's Day," was a legal obligation.[13] Commager judged rightly that the American brand of Christianity
was conventional rather than creative, that "religion prospered
while theology went slowly bankrupt." [14] The Americans
naturalized God as they naturalized other concepts. "Because
they distrusted arbitrary authority, they qualified his omnipotence by reading into it respect for law." [15] Civil piety and
"religion-in-general" grew up alongside church and sectarian
religion.[16]

The Cambridge (England) political scientist D. W. Brogan, writing after World War II, reached the same conclusion. He considered it "natural that American political society should rely on verbal affirmations, on formal organization of loyalty, of national feeling, should see allegiance, not as an accident of birth, but as an exercise of will, should preach . . . *a political religion,* set up *a political church* outside which there is, in America, no salvation." [17] Charles A. Reich—in an exciting contemporary work of uneven value, *The Greening of America*—judges that "structure, or established lawful procedures, comes to nothing without consciousness. By itself, the imposition of structure is useless." [18] The Weimar Republic had a liberal, written constitution, but the German temper of mind and a debilitating socio-economic situation permitted Adolf Hitler to come to power *constitutionally.* A century earlier the Prussian military state had grown up under the constitution of the Holy Roman Empire.

Lord Bryce, English Ambassador to Washington in the 1880s, was impressed by the American's pride in his political institutions. He noted that the first question which Americans addressed to European travelers was: "What do you think of our institutions?" [19] The American revered his democratic society and his republican form of government; he considered them incomparable, unparalleled, and unique. He was convinced that everyone should emulate his form of government and accept his style of life. Bryce himself was impressed with the American political institutions: "They represent an experiment in the rule of the multitude, tried on a scale unprecedentedly vast, and the results of which everyone is concerned to watch. And yet they are something more than an experiment, for they are believed to disclose and display the type of institutions towards which, as by a law of fate, the rest of civilized mankind is forced to move, some with swifter, others with slower, but all with unresting feet." [20]

Seven decades later D. W. Brogan judged that "the American institution [political] has been a success; so Americans think, so the reflective portion of non-American mankind must concede. But because that Constitution has been a success, it has acquired in the eyes of . . . 'the People of the United States,' a claim to reverence, to uncritical acceptance, that has no parallel in the world." [21] The American was justified in his pride in his political institutions but arrogantly naïve in his assumption that they were perfectly and forever adequate.

The American historian Henry Steele Commager, writing at the same time as D. W. Brogan (1950), observed that the American's optimism, in spite of his profession of Calvinism, was indefatigable: "Whatever they, the Americans, may have said, or sung, they preferred this life to the next, and when they imagined heaven, they thought of it as operating under an American Constitution." [22] Throughout the later eighteenth and nineteenth centuries the American regarded the United States as a paradise, not a purgatory.

Earlier, Lord Bryce had observed that "America changes so fast that every few years a new crop of books is needed to describe the new face which things have put on, the new problems that have appeared, the new ideas germinating among her people, the new and unexpected developments for evil as well as for good of which her established institutions have been found capable." [23] But one aspect of American life, Bryce judged, had not changed since the days when Tocqueville examined American social, political, and religious institutions.

> Christianity is in fact understood to be, though not the legally established religion, yet the national religion. So far from thinking their commonwealth Godless, the Americans conceive that the religious character of a government consists in nothing but the religious beliefs of the individual citizens, and the conformity of their conduct to that belief. They deem the general acceptance of Christianity as a special object of the Divine favor.[24]

This deep-seated religious impulse remained strong at the dawn of the twentieth century when Theodore Roosevelt, seeing the American as the new "national" come-of-age and the "strenuous" leader in world affairs, bombastically trumpeted the necessity to embark on a national quest for social justice. The notion that "trust-busting Teddy" was simply a political opportunist who capitalized on the muckraking reports of Ida Tarbell, Herbert Croly, Lincoln Steffens, Upton Sinclair, Ray Stannard Baker, *et al.,* does not square with the man's religious training and personal commitment to justice as he understood it. Reared in the Dutch Reformed Church (strict Calvinist), Roosevelt was convinced that justice is God's primary attribute and that God expects justice to be done among his people.[25] Roosevelt, commenting on Micah 6:8, observed that the Lord required justice *first* in his followers; mercy and humility were poor seconds on his religious-political agenda.[26] Roosevelt desired ardently that justice should roll down from the mountains across America and over the world. He envisioned America as the leader in a righteous crusade and relished his privileged position as President in advancing America's new place of world leadership.[27] The White House, Teddy proclaimed joyously, was "a bully pulpit!"

Chauvinistic, bombastic, yet moderate in domestic politics, Theodore Roosevelt had a sense of justice which not only led him to dramatize trust-busting but also constrained him to challenge local situations which perpetrated injustice. For example, the Japanese victories against Russia in 1904-1905 awakened anxiety about the "yellow peril" on the west coast. Late in 1906 the San Francisco Board of Education acted to segregate the ninety-three Japanese children in the city in a separate school. Japan was offended. President Roosevelt, incensed by California's exclusivism, denounced the San Francisco action in his annual message to Congress in 1906 as a "wicked absurdity." He got the action reversed; most Americans applauded his action. [28]

The period from Roosevelt's presidency to the outbreak of World War I was the Progressive Era, a season when the American citizens and their elected representatives engaged in a quest for social justice. Reforms in business and politics were effected. Public aspirations outran political achievements, but the efforts at reform were significant as well as earnest. The American was determined to correct the more serious abuses which had grown up in the preceding generation of industrializing America and making money. From 1870 to 1900 Henry George, Edward Bellamy, Upton Sinclair, and others had made searing critiques of America's dehumanized society and oligarchical government. From the turn of the century to the eve of World War I, politicians like Robert M. LaFollette, William Jennings Bryan, Theodore Roosevelt, and

Woodrow Wilson—guided by the intellectual social critics and prodded by the muckrakers—helped to correct a welter of social and political ills by reform laws. It was during this period that the reform tradition in America underwent a fundamental change. It moved from the dogma of natural rights toward a relativistic, environmentalist, and pragmatic view of the world. There are different opinions why the change occurred. Some critics identify it with "a new readiness to use government (particularly the federal government) as an instrument of popular control. Others associate it with an abandonment of the old populist distrust of large-scale institutions, like corporations, and an acceptance of the inevitability of the concentration of wealth and power." [29] But the American was shedding the image of independent frontiersman and altering the individualistic Protestant ethic at the end of the nineteenth century.

Who the American was, and is, continued to be articulated by what Americans said, did, tried, and dreamed, no less than by intellectual critics, reformers, politicians, and social historians. The "Robber Barons" (Rockefeller, Harriman, Hill, etc.) of the late nineteenth century had grown into the more dangerous corporate giants who, through mergers and interlocking directorates, controlled vast economic empires which crushed people. Reform politicians, leading and following the cries of the masses for economic justice, enacted significant legislation which reasserted the Federal Government's power to regulate business for the commonweal—the Sherman Anti-Trust Act, the Pure Food and Drug Act, the direct election of senators, the graduated income tax, etc.

America did join Britain briefly for a venture in imperialism after the Spanish-American War, but empire-making as a *conscious political* venture was a brief interlude. America granted the Philippines independence in 1945. Alaska and Hawaii became the forty-ninth and fiftieth states respectively in 1958 and 1961. Economic imperialism, on the other hand, was a different issue. The troubles let loose by "dollar diplomacy" are still sitting on America's front porch. The Rockefeller Report on Latin America in 1969 reminded America freshly of that reality.

But in 1917 the American—egalitarian, religious, legalistic— was more self-righteous than imperialistic as he joined in Wilson's crusade to "make the world safe for democracy." Tragically, that goal was not achieved. Wearied, disillusioned, cynical, Americans balked at joining the League of Nations and took time out from world affairs for self-indulgence in the 1920s, reexamined their political foundations during the soul-searing economic debacle of the 1930s, and laid the foundations for the welfare state.

Franklin Roosevelt's clarion call to crusade against "the malefactors of great wealth," master the Depression, avenge the day of infamy and—in concert with Britain—save Western civilization from the Nazi barbarians captivated most Americans and raised their spirits. But he and his fellow citizens glossed over the violence between the classes which came into focus in the Bonus March on Washington (1933) and the hatred between the races which erupted in the riots in Detroit (1944). The cancers of class conflict and racial prejudice in American society were ignored.

In the mid-1940s a majority of Americans followed Harry Truman, "the captain with the mighty heart," as he guided the nation in rebuilding war-ravaged western Europe, especially West Germany, and containing the "colossus" of the East, Communism. Later, Americans cheered as Dwight Eisenhower negotiated a cease-fire in Korea, allowed a former president of the Federal Council of Churches, John Foster Dulles, to play the politics of morality to the hilt, and suggested that America was on the edge of the Kingdom of God. The Russian's Sputnik, the deterioration in the quality of American life, and a nationwide racial revolution shocked most Americans into taking stock anew. John Kennedy, in a futuristic inaugural address, challenged his fellow citizens to positive acceptance of the world as it is and the burden of improving it wherever they could: "Ask not what your country can do for you, but what you can do for your country." His winsome appeal persuaded many Americans, especially the young, to fresh social involvement. But President Kennedy's charisma, maturing social consciousness, decisiveness, and futurism were ripped from American society by death-laden bullets in the American city of Dallas. Even so, President Kennedy's thousand days produced as much legislation as was enacted in the whole of Franklin Roosevelt's first term.[30]

The spirit of reform, rooted in religious fervor, has been a powerful force in the American's national life. He has considered his political institutions to be inviolate. With uncritical faith in the presumed perfection and supposed universal desirability of those institutions, the American has attempted to reform social ills at home and abroad. This impulse has waned at times, and it has frequently been shortsighted, one-sided, coercive, naïve. But the impulse to perfect the American way of life and to remake the world in his own image has been a dominant strand in the American character.

The American has accomplished political and social reform in the past, but is he willing to pay the price of creative change? What course will he pursue when his confidence in his political institutions wanes? In the context of these questions, we shall examine several new factors which, cutting across the American's nineteenth-century life-style, delineate his contemporary character.

The Bewildered American

A fundamental change in American society occurred during the 1890s. That decade was a watershed; America changed from a rural-agricultural nation to an urban-industrial nation. From colonial days space had been a key factor in the molding of American culture. But the geographical frontier disapapeared before the turn of the nineteenth century. In 1890 the superintendent of the United States Census made one of the momentous observations in American history: "Up to and including 1880 the country had a frontier of settlement, but at present the unsettled area has been so broken into . . . that there can hardly be said to be a frontier line. In the discussion of its extent, its westward movement, etc., it cannot, therefore, any longer have a place in the census reports." [31] The American's socio-economic safety valve was gone.

From the beginning native Americans and immigrants had associated land with freedom and space with opportunity.[32] But as early as the 1880s free farmland had become relatively scarce, the fencing of open range had occurred in spite of range wars, much of the virgin forest had been turned into stumps, and once rich mine sites were marked by ghost towns.[33] Horace Greeley's "Go West, young man" was even then, in 1880, a haunting echo from the past. But new frontiers of science, business management, and technology emerged which, ventured upon, produced new wealth, altered attitudes, modified mores, and stirred social conflict. The disappearance of the geographic frontier and its influence, together with the end of their natural preoccupation with continental United States, allowed Americans to come of age in a diverse world community.

On the far side of 1890 was an agricultural people, preoccupied with domestic problems and conforming to the economic, political, and moral principles dominant in the seventeenth and eighteenth centuries. It was an America still in the making physically, socially, and politically; an America that was idealistic, optimistic, self-reliant—convinced that its character and destiny were unique.[34] On the twentieth-century side of 1890 was an urban-industrial America, inextricably involved in world economy and politics; "troubled with the problems that had long been thought peculiar to the Old World; experiencing profound changes. . . ; and trying to accommodate its traditional institutions and habits of thought to conditions new and in part alien." [35] This change, underway before the Civil War, actually had helped to precipitate that conflict (the industrial North *vs.* the agrarian South).

The process of change was not new to the American at the close of the nineteenth century. But the tempo of change accelerated so rapidly during the twentieth century that by 1970 he had become frightened; would his political and social

institutions be adaptable in this turbulent technological society? Although the change in the American's material situation after 1890 was convulsive, he adapted his social and political institutions only slowly in spite of four wars, an economic
debacle, a racial revolution, a class revolution, and a youth
revolution.[36] Many—especially many blacks, poverty-ridden
people, young people, and some intellectuals—questioned
whether the traditional institutions of American society were
adequate for human life in the new age. Herbert Marcuse,
Eldridge Cleaver, and others announced loudly the end of
the first evolutionary stage of American society.[37] In the
spring of 1970 David McReynolds, field secretary of the War
Resisters' League and author of *We Have Been Invaded by
the Twenty-First Century,* analyzed America's current situation in this fashion: "Are we in the beginning of a Second
American Revolution? Yes and no. Paradox: revolutions can
occur only after they have occurred. Marx's call for revolution
in 1848 was based on the revolutionary changes that had
already occurred—the emergence of the proletariat. . . . Revolutions do not occur because of revolutionaries but because of
massive social tensions that demand change, combined with a
political establishment unwilling or unable to make those
changes. That situation exists today in America." [38]

In the symposium which invited Mr. McReynold's response
to the question, "Are we in the middle of the Second American Revolution?" Richard H. Rovere, author of the "Letter
from Washington" column in the *New Yorker,* opined: "So
many things are out of joint in this country that if they were
all, or nearly all, set right, or nearly right, the changes, by

whatever means accomplished, would constitute a revolution of great magnitude." [39]

Paul Cowan, former Peace Corps member and author of *The Making of an Un-American,* participating in the same symposium, argued like the Secessionists of 1860: "Maybe our history has injected a poison into our blood stream that forces us to be violent. Then, I would rather see Kansans fight Oklahomans than be part of a country where Kansans and Oklahomans are drafted into an army which forces them to drop bombs on Cambodians, Laotians, Vietnamese, their houses, schools, and hospitals. My slogan is: Dissolution before decay!" [40]

The American of Crevecoeur, Tocqueville, and Bryce had been emasculated by an "escalation of technology to an autonomous, self-determining system. . . . The Manhattan Project put man (including the American) at the mercy of his technological genius. . . . Massive bureaucracies applied rational principles of control to things and people." [41] Technology had produced a society, culture, and political structure radically different from those of nineteenth-century idealistic America. In those decades culture was based on futurism. The political society rested on an egalitarian respect for liberty which was motivated by the Christian religion (Arminianism).

C. P. Snow, British scientist-novelist-politician, in a series of lectures at Harvard University, delineated the chasmic difference between the past (1776-1945) and the present (1945-1972): "One of the most bizarre features of any advanced industrial society in our time is that *the cardinal choices have to be made by a handful of men; in secret,* and, at least in legal form, by men who cannot have a first-hand knowledge of what those choices depend upon or what their results may be." [42]

This specter has become especially frightening because America is changing from a society of individuals to a society of numbers. Americans are by all odds the most numbered, the most numerated, the most frequently and variously counted people on earth.[43] The young have Selective Service numbers. All wage earners have Social Security numbers. Millions have credit card numbers. Most people over sixteen have drivers' license numbers. Everyone has a zip code number. A census is taken each decade.

Statistics have been a significant part of the American political system since 1787, when one of the compromises on the Federal Constitution provided for a two-house legislature, one of which allowed the people to be represented according to their numbers. Daniel Boorstin is convinced that the members of American communities are no longer held together by shared political dogmas or religious traditions but by "a shared consciousness, a shared awareness. People now think of themselves as members of groups and classes which were unimagined only a century ago." [44] America has become a fragmented society. Andrew Hacker calls America a nation of "two hundred million egos." [45]

Philip Slater, professor of sociology at Brandeis University, has written brilliantly, if pessimistically, about American culture at the breaking point.[46] Speaking of a traveler returning from a season abroad, Slater suggests that the traveler, on reentering America, "is struck first of all by the grim monotony of American facial expressions—hard, surly, and bitter —and by the aura of deprivation that informs them." [47]

John W. Gardner, agonizing over this deterioration in the quality of American life, wrote in 1968 that " 'having enough of everything' isn't enough. If it were, the large number of Americans who have been able to indulge their whims on a scale unprecedented in history would be telling one another of their unparalleled serenity and bliss instead of trading tranquilizer prescriptions." [48] Slater is convinced that American society is devoted to "the pursuit of loneliness." [49]

These sharp images of the American are diametrically opposed to the buoyant, graceful images projected by Crevecoeur, Tocqueville, and Bryce. They are essentially different from the strong images sketched by Commager and Brogan two short decades ago. The America of Crevecoeur, Tocqueville, and Bryce is gone forever, and the society that replaced it has again changed radically during the last two decades. The American was convinced for a century and a half that he could solve any problem. After World War I he shifted from the age of confidence to the age of anxiety. Currently, he is drifting to the edge of despair and impotence. His spirit sags to his bootstraps. He has little confidence in himself or his sociopolitical institutions.

Scintillating idealism, brash confidence, and a warm sense of brotherhood are qualities which have been eroded steadily in American life during the last half century. The American's eager confidence in the superiority of his political institutions is severely damaged. During the Depression "Brother, can you spare a dime?" was a debilitating plea from Maine to California. Breadlines, the "Bonus March," executives peddling apples, starving coal miners, and depressed migrant laborers turned the economic depression into a spiritual depression. Nonetheless, the American political institutions were adapted and made to function, and the American went on to new heights in material achievement—but the quality of human life did not improve.[50]

America had changed. World War II gave technology the reason and money to develop. The bomb drop in 1945 and the subsequent rampaging technology overwhelmed America's social institutions, threatened mankind with extinction, and, paradoxically, encouraged Africa, Asia, and Latin America to seek places in the sun. In a world where much, but not enough, had been achieved in the socio-political arena, technology threatened annihilation for all or promised the survival of islands of opulence and frustration in seas of poverty and alienation.[51]

The quality of American life was downgraded for millions, while millions more, discovering they had known neither quality nor quantity, determined to seize at least the latter. Looting during the riots in the cities in the mid-1960s reflected not only the poor American's rising expectations but also his materialism. Whether American society had become affluent with pockets of poverty (as John Kenneth Galbraith argued), or poor with pockets of affluence (as Nicholas Kisburg maintained), the American was getting more goods in the 1950s and 60s while enjoying them less. Meantime, his confidence in his democratic government was being dealt added heavy blows by the Kennedy-King-Kennedy assassinations in 1963 and 1968 and the widening credibility gaps which undermined the Johnson Administration and threatened the

Nixon Administration. An ineffable sadness settled over many Americans during the 60s. The middle-aged citizen grieved over his young who disrupted college campuses and in some places died violently. He brooded over the grievous fact that 70,000 young men had left the country rather than serve in the American military services. Thousands more who stayed protested vigorously from coast to coast, many accepting jail sentences rather than military service. Everywhere in America, pollution endangered human life in the country's once healthful, scenic, virgin environment. And responsible men admitted publicly that economically poor Americans, white and black, were not getting justice in American courts.[52]

Presently, millions of Americans, especially blacks and youth, question whether contemporary social and political institutions can be altered radically enough to serve human needs effectively. But few at any age inquire seriously whether man-as-he-is is able to recast his institutions to serve persons and thereafter administer them responsibly. Is it possible to be a responsible self in an urban-technological society? The American has barely perceived that there is a clear relationship not only between law and morality but also between morality and law. New laws, however equitable in theory, will not work unless a majority of citizens want them to work. A democratic government can be better, but not much better, than the mass of people which constitutes it. The American himself needs human values, humane goals, self-confidence, and a God who does not fail. Because technological man is becoming a worldwide phenomenon, not only Americans but people everywhere are under social constraint to search out new dynamics as well as new structures for the humanization of mankind.

Charles Reich is convinced that "there is a revolution coming. It will not be like revolutions of the past. It will originate with the individual and with culture, and it will change the political structure only as its final act. It will not require violence to succeed, and it cannot be successfully resisted by violence. . . . It promises a higher reason, a more human community, and a new and liberated individual. Its ultimate creation will be a new and enduring wholeness and beauty— a renewed relationship of man to himself, to other men, to society, to nature, and to the land." [53]

If that is to happen, civilized man must pull himself together, develop a new consciousness, and boldly fashion humane policies and procedures to keep his world from being blown to pieces by nuclear missiles, fragmented by disruptive minorities, shattered into atomistic social units by distrust between the races, the generations, and the sexes, or smothered by poverty, population, and pollution. The American can produce long-range missiles, but he has done little to better the socio-economic conditions among the revolutionary peoples of Africa, Asia, and Latin America. He can transplant human hearts successfully, but he has not yet learned to cope with the power politics which divide Europe. He can expand his national economy, but he has not eradicated mass poverty in his own land. The human equation is as important in building the good society as the structural-institutional equation. Human problems always become social in scope, but they are never simply social. Without human values and responsible selves to fashion and administer flexible institutional structures which are designed to help people to be human, America will become totalitarian as the only viable means for keeping order in a pluralistic society where classes and races are alienated from one another. But the American tradition is favorable; "radicalism is part of the secret history of the United States." [54]

"Middle America" (the middle-class, middle-aged, substantially white population) is presently disturbed by the rapid social and moral changes in American life. This solid segment of society has been encouraged and goaded (as was the South during the 1850s) to focus its frustrations and fury on students, militant blacks, welfare recipients, and the liberal intelligentsia. But instead of a new conservative majority emerging from Middle America, which Barry Goldwater still envisions, Middle Americans continue to support the goals of a liberal political society. They demonstrated that again in the 1970 congressional elections. Their deepest concern focuses on the current lack of community, personal loneliness, and faltering confidence in their political and social traditions. Dynamic political leadership, rather than bureaucratic management at the top, could contribute to bridging that gap.

Because the Middle American is a take-charge fellow, he is anxious and suspicious because he is not in charge of change.[55] He is experiencing difficulty in learning to live with change which outruns his conscious expectations. Any political leadership which plays on the Middle American's fears rather than awakening his hopes serves neither him nor the country.[56] Most Middle Americans still have a reservoir of sympathy, compassion, and charity. Tocqueville's and Bryce's "American" has vanished, but his blood courses through the veins of the Middle American. He needs to be challenged and cared for, not catered to or manipulated in his political society and religious community. His confidence in his democratic state has been damaged; it has not been destroyed. His confidence can be restored if he is persuaded to participate in the cultural revolution.

The American, in three violence-packed centuries, conquered a wilderness, settled a continent, robbed the unassimilated Indian of his humanity, enslaved and then ghettoed the blacks, fashioned an optimistic, self-righteous life-style, and adapted his social and political institutions to change. In the course of this complex, action-crammed process, he demonstrated that he loves freedom for himself and, under inner and external constraint, will provide or allow it for others. During the twentieth century the American fought a war to make the world safe for democracy; provided the muscle to stop the totalitarian onslaught of the Nazi and Japanese expansionists; took the initiative (and then lost it) in establishing a world organization of nations; expended billions of dollars to rebuild western Europe; and contained Communism in Greece, East Germany, Korea, and Cuba. During the 1930s and again in the 1960s the American, functioning unevenly within the framework of the law, responded to the two most intensive social revolutions in single decades of his turbulent history—a socio-economic revolution and a racial-cultural revolution. He weathered the first; in the second, he is sailing in rough waters.

The white American loves *his* freedom; that is written in his history. His dislike of discipline is a firm strand in his character. The American is a true child of the Enlightenment, which stressed man's freedom from authority, the goodness of man, and the democratic process.[57] He questions any authority which limits his freedom unless he can see that it benefits him directly. The American—individualistic, experimental, pragmatic, inventive—reacts immaturely to authority. "Two world wars had not induced in him either a sense of sin or that awareness of evil almost instinctive with most Old World peoples—war had not taught him discipline or respect for authority." [58]

There are times and seasons when revolution becomes inevitable. History confirms that the American Revolution was one of those times. The Declaration of Independence provided the rational-pragmatic description of political conditions which made revolution necessary. The Americans have been in the throes of cultural revolution since 1945. But, as Arthur M. Schlesinger, Jr., observed in 1970, the necessity for violent political revolution has not yet developed in America. He judges that "however deplorable the present situation of the United States, it can hardly be said that we have exhausted nonrevolutionary remedies. Still the fashion of revolutionary talk . . . ought to convey a warning to our leaders. . . . Should the Administration thus continue to make our institutions more rigid and regressive, our internal divisions will certainly deepen. As John F. Kennedy once said, 'Those who make peaceful revolution impossible will make violent revolution inevitable.' But also, in the words of Adam Smith, there is a lot of ruin in a country." [59]

Like his fellow citizen, the American churchman also loves his freedom. He is undisciplined, indisposed to accept authority. He has a dull sense of sin and little awareness of evil as a deep-seated reality in life. In fact, the American churchman's tradition of anti-authoritarian individualism dulls his sensitivity to the serious nature of egocentricity in himself and others—and the self-serving character of all institutions. He is loath to accept any external standard of judgment upon his person, ideas, actions. Until God's sovereignty is recognized and acknowledged in and by the church, that institution will be an adjunct of the state and a handmaiden of culture; civic piety and religion-in-general will be America's religion.

Gibson Winter argues that "America has been nurtured by two faith communities—a community of natural right and a community of biblical faith, the faith community finding expression in Jewish, Protestant, and Catholic forms. The civil religion of rights and the confessional faiths—were ultimately grounded in trust in diety. . . . We now seem to be at a stage where the confessional heritage is a last hope for renewal and liberation; but this requires a retrieval of the religious heritage." [60] That religious heritage is deep-set in the American experience. But would the American people who had solved many baffling and even bloody problems in the past recover confidence in the viability of their institutions? Would they, having adapted to so much so rapidly after 1940—albeit uncertainly, irritably, dispiritedly—adapt further to the increased tempo of social revolution in the 1970s? Would they retrieve their heritage of affirmation? These questions are the foci in subsequent chapters.

Chapter 4

DISSENT IN AMERICA

If all mankind minus one, were of one opinion, and only one person were of the contrary opinion, mankind would be no more justified in silencing that one person, than he, if he had the power, would be justified in silencing mankind. . . . If the opinion is right, they are deprived of the opportunity of exchanging error for truth; if wrong, they lose, what is almost as great a benefit, the clearer perception and livelier impression of truth, produced by its collision with error.

—*John Stuart Mill, On Liberty (1859)*

American democracy has undergone a series of fundamental changes in its philosophical presuppositions over the last two centuries. During the seventeenth century a stern Calvinism—"In Adam's Fall, we sinned all"—pervaded American political thought and action. The Founding Fathers, deeply influenced by neoclassicism and the writings of John Locke, were, nonetheless, Calvinistic in their view of human possibilities: "Every man by Nature has the seeds of Tyranny deeply implanted within." [1]

This rigorous appraisal of human nature influenced the framers of the Constitution to produce a tripartite government larded with checks and balances. It dominated American political thought until the time of Andrew Jackson (1828), when a more sanguine estimate of man's possibilities slipped into American political thought. The sources of this new optimism were multiple: "The new mystique of democracy and the common man, welling up from the American and French Revolutions; from the beneficent and harmonizing role newly assigned to individual self-interest by the laissez-faire economics of Adam Smith; from the passionate new romantic faith in human innocency, in self-reliance, and in the perfectability of man, a faith stimulated by English poetry, French political theory, and German philosophy; and, above all from the new circumstances of life and opportunity in nineteenth-century America." [2]

The Civil War throttled America's surging optimism, but only briefly. Optimism was a dynamic in the Populist movement of the 1880s; it invigorated the Progressive movement in the early 1900s. The "social gospel" and John Dewey's democratic pragmatism owed much to this pervasive buoyancy of spirit and developing civic piety. That optimism survived the wholesale killing of World War I but was corroded by the Depression, World War II, and the affluent 1950s. The cold war and the social revolution of the 1960s took an added toll. The citizenry, buffeted by radical change on all fronts, lost heart steadily after John Kennedy's assassination. No President thereafter exhibited an ability to awaken—as Kennedy had—what Harold Laski called "the dynamic of democracy" latent in the American public. Meantime, America's optimism had been punctured ideologically by a corps of intellectual critics: Reinhold and Richard Niebuhr, Jacques Ellul, Herbert Marcuse, James Baldwin, Martin Luther King, and Eldridge Cleaver. During the mid-twentieth century the

American changed from a man who was convinced that he could solve every problem to one who felt he could solve few, if any, problems.

As recently as 1920 a report of the Federal Council of Churches' Committee on the War and the Religious Outlook had declared with buoyant optimism that "the entire social order must be Christianized. . . . Is such an ideal practicable? Beautiful though it be, can it ever be anything more than another Utopia? To this question the Christian answer is definite and unmistakable. This ideal can, indeed, be realized." [3]

But that climate of national expectation had changed radically by the 1970s. Extremists were insisting that governmental structures were woefully antiquated; revolution was their avowed goal.[4] Moderate reformers were hard-pressed to know what to do; the political structures frustrated their efforts to effect change.[5] Ultra-conservatives waved the flag and shouted for "lawnorder" with little awareness that order rests on social justice.[6] Dissent—radical, moderate, ultra-conservative—surged through American politics during the decade of the 1960s.

American Precedents for Dissent

Dissent and violence, we have discovered, are not new on the American scene. Both have been used often in our past, quite purposefully, and a full reckoning with that fact is a necessary factor in any realistic national self-image.[7] The nation was settled by people who were unwilling or unable to adapt to the social, economic, and religious status quo in the England of their day and, after 1650, in other European countries. Once settled on these shores some of them continued to dissent from violence against the mind which was frequent in New England.[8] As we have noted, Captain John Smith of the Virginia Colony established a police state at Jamestown to preserve that settlement in its early years. During the Civil War, Abraham Lincoln imitated Captain Smith in several high-handed acts. One of his boldest coercive deeds was the suspension of the writ of *habeus corpus* to keep the North united in its war with the South.[9] Treatment of conscientious objectors in World War I was harsh. The forced resettlement of Japanese Americans at the outset of World War II was retaliatory and violent.[10]

The records of the Pilgrims reveal that there was dissent before they landed on American shores. Aboard the *Mayflower* anchored off Plymouth Rock, some grumbled against the decisions that were being made about the place of settlement, the procedure for it, and the proposed government of it. The Puritan commonwealth practiced thought control. It accused several women of witchcraft because they did not conform to the accepted social and religious patterns which the commonwealth had decreed. Several of these independent women were hanged. Roger Williams, arguing for the disestablishment of religion a century and a half before Jefferson, was driven from the Massachusetts Bay colony in mid-winter because his views were antithetic to those of the Puritan theocracy.[11] Quakers were unwelcome and abused in most colonies throughout the seventeenth century. Only Rhode Island and Pennsylvania welcomed religious dissenters. But even in those colonies the Quakers and other peace-loving sects experienced social pressures.

Religious, social, economic, and political dissenters peopled the colonies in every year of the intolerant seventeenth century. The first full-scale rebellion was led by Nathaniel Bacon in Virginia in 1676. Bacon's frontiersmen, dissatisfied with the government's inept protection against the Indians, moved first against the red men and then against the royal governor, Sir William Berkeley, and the Virginia Assembly. Bacon's premature death prevented a violent confrontation between the people of the west and the seaboard government.[12] Because voting and office-holding in colonial America were limited to property holders, uprisings like Bacon's occurred in Maryland in 1676 and 1689; in South Carolina in 1681 and 1719; in North Carolina (the Regulators) in 1771. Frontiersmen known as the Paxton Boys marched on the capital of Pennsylvania in 1764.[13]

During the 1760s political dissent spread throughout the colonies, the strongest centers being Massachusetts and Virginia. Patrick Henry's "Give me liberty or give me death" was dissent which bordered on treason. The Boston Tea Party was the wanton destruction of private property. The shot fired at Concord was outright rebellion. Piety as well as patriotism motivated the dissent. The Great Awakening which swept America after 1740 loosed a wave of religious excitement which cascaded through the colonies with an immediate effect on American *political* life.[14]

The young republic was barely launched before it faced a frontier uprising in western Pennsylvania (1794). The government, having enacted an excise tax, was challenged by the

Scotch-Irish in western Pennsylvania, who refused to pay the tax on the whiskey they made from their grain. Transportation was inadequate to the eastern markets; it was not profitable for these farmers to transport their corn to market so they turned their grain into whiskey. The federal excise tax hit them in their pocketbooks. Refusing to pay, they ran the federal tax collectors out of town, having tarred and feathered several. The Federal Government could not ignore these acts of defiance. President Washington called up 15,000 troops under the command of Alexander Hamilton. The federalized militia marched as far as Bedford, Pennsylvania, before the rebels decided to accept the authority of the government.[15]

In 1798 the Kentucky and Virginia Resolutions—enacted to protest the Federal Government's Alien and Sedition Acts[16] —declared for states' rights, arguing that the states had the constitutional right to nullify any federal legislation which they deemed to be unconstitutional. In 1814 the New Englanders, fiercely at odds with their Federal Government over the war with England and the interruption of their lucrative commerce, gathered at Hartford, Connecticut, to discuss self-defense because the British were occupying the coast of Maine. The Federal Government, reacting to New England's dissent from the War, had declined to provide troops. Although the meetings at Hartford, Connecticut, were secret, it is generally agreed that the representatives were considering the possibility of New England's secession from the Union. These seditious plans, however, were nipped in the bud by Jackson's victory at New Orleans and the signing of the peace treaty at Paris.[17] Throughout the War certain New Englanders had clamored openly for a separate peace with England.

The decade following the War of 1812 was an "era of good feeling" in American political society; dissent was low-key. But Jacksonian "democracy" ended that interlude. From 1830 to 1860 dissent escalated and spread. Although there was co-operation among the Americans on many fronts, those three decades were marked by individualism, provincialism, vigilantism, and egalitarianism. Tocqueville observed in 1831 that Americans pounce "upon equality as booty." Disagreement, dissent, disorder, and violence ran high as the nation exploded to its present borders, as urbanization set in, as a distinct American culture took shape. The vicious outburst of anti-Irish, anti-Negro, and anti-Abolitionist rioting in the 1830s provided Abraham Lincoln, at twenty-eight, with the reason for his first significant public speech. Addressing the young men of Springfield, Illinois, in January, 1838, Lincoln deplored the violence and lawlessness then abroad in the nation. "If destruction be our lot, we must ourselves be its author and finisher." [18] Actually, the bulk of American violence "has been initiated with a 'conservative' bias. It has been unleashed against Abolitionists, Catholics, radicals, workers and labor organizers, Negroes, Orientals, and other ethnic or racial or ideological minorities, and has been used ostensibly to protect the American, the Southerner, the white Protestant, or simply the established middle-class way of life and morals." [19]

Lincoln's maiden speech was inspired by the mob action in Alton, Illinois, in 1837, which had ended in the murder of Elijah P. Lovejoy, an antislavery editor. Added to the attacks on Abolitionists in the 1830s and 40s and 50s, the Know-Nothing party (anti-Catholic) fostered the use of violence in keeping foreign-born voters from the polls and harassing

them generally. Clashes between them and Democratic organizations, bloody and lethal, occurred in all American cities.
The members of the Know-Nothing party were held together
by their hatred for the Catholic Church.[20] Added to the
nativist riots were those of Negroes against whites (Nat
Turner, 1831) and the Texas slave insurrection (1860), which
in turn incited violent acts of white retaliation. In the New
York City draft riots (five days in July, 1863, during which
1,200 persons were killed and property damage ran to millions of dollars), racial tension between the Irish and the
Negroes was more of a precipitating factor than anti-war
feeling.[21]

In addition to the violent outbursts against Irish, Negroes,
and Abolitionists, there was wide dissent about the establishment of public schools in America. Those who were well-to-
do sent their children to private schools or employed private
tutors; they saw no need to help the children of laborers and
farmers get an education. Although public schools flourished
in New England and New York and the upper Mississippi
Valley, they did not prosper in Pennsylvania, New Jersey,
throughout the South, or on the frontier. It was not until
1860 that most states in the North had established a tax-
supported school program; the South and the frontier had
none. But public education, while it contributed to destroying
caste in a democratic state, was neither academically excellent
nor objective. Adding a fourth "R" (religion), it fostered a
watered-down Protestant piety.[22]

Dissent and violence were as much a national sport as
politics and poker in the America of 1830 to 1860. Some citizens dissented from the use of alcoholic beverages, and the

demand for prohibition began. Others dissented from the harsh treatment which the mentally ill received, and efforts to reform the asylums were launched. Many dissented from denominationalism, and sectarianism thrived. Others dissented from the cruel treatment accorded prisoners, and the beginnings of prison reform were discernible. Some rebelled totally against contemporary society itself and proceeded to set up utopian communities of their own. Recalling the emotional excitement of 1840, Ralph Waldo Emerson wrote, "We were all a little mad that winter. Not a man of us that did not have a plan for some new Utopia in his pocket." Everywhere dissent reigned and violence raged in the bustling, half-formed, expanding nation. The most vigorous dissent movement between 1830 and 1860 centered in northeastern United States among people who opposed the social institution of slavery. The underground railway for runaway slaves was a grass-roots evidence of the vigor of that dissent.

From the beginning the Quakers, the disciples of Roger Williams, and other humanitarians had opposed slavery. But dissent went into high gear after 1831 when William Lloyd Garrison established his influential *Liberator,* one of the most incendiary periodicals ever published in American society. Garrison worked not only for the abolition of slavery but for the abolition of capital punishment, the ending of the imprisonment for debt, for international peace, and for women's rights. He declared publicly that the Constitution is "a covenant with death and an agreement with Hell." In the presence of fellow townsmen he burned a copy of the historic document. Wendell Phillips became an Abolitionist the day he watched a mob drag Garrison down Court Street in Boston in 1835. Southerners also reacted violently against Garrison; an anti-Abolitionist movement sprang up throughout the South. This collision course between dissenters and status-quoers, each group convinced that their cause was righteous, ended in "the irrepressible conflict." But civil rights for blacks in a predominantly white political society were not settled by that holocaust. The partial solution effected in the 1860s loosed subsequent waves of bitter dissent over the next hundred years—Reconstruction, Ku Klux Klan, socio-economic racism, civil rights, black power, separatism.

The industrialization of America, hastened by the Civil War, produced new groups of dissenters: the farmers in the West, the growing army of urban-centered factory laborers, and the general public who reacted angrily against the industrial and economic monopolies which burgeoned after the Civil War. The Populist revolt, which united the farmers and some laborers in the demand that the Federal Government regulate industry and the railroads, sparked several decades of clamorous dissent and partial reforms. But it was labor which rode into public view on continuing acts of violence when the public as well as industry begrudged them any real improvement in their harsh working conditions.

Prior to the Civil War labor was disorganized; it relied on utopian schemes and abstract ideas that drifted in from Europe. During and after the Civil War it turned to trade-union-ism and collective bargaining. Labor's first significant growth was under the auspices of the Knights of Labor, founded in 1869 by a Philadelphia tailor, Uriah S. Stephens. The Knights attempted to organize the workers of America into a single union under centralized control. Their policies were liberal:

men and women, blacks and whites, skilled and unskilled, merchants and farmers were invited to join. "Only liquor dealers, professional gamblers, lawyers, and bankers were excluded." [23] The Puritan ethic was still pervasive.

Initially, the Knights of Labor experienced tremendous growth since the time for labor organization was long overdue. Simultaneously, nonpolitical trade unions of skilled workers and socialist unions also flourished, ten having come into existence during the Civil War. In 1886 the workers in America joined in a general strike for the eight-hour day. The event that galvanized this nationwide uprising was the Haymarket bomb explosion in Chicago. On May 3, 1886, the police had killed and wounded a number of labor demonstrators who were participating in the long drawn-out strike against the McCormack Harvester Company. On May 4, the police again broke into a mass meeting which was then protesting that massacre; someone threw a bomb which injured sixty persons and killed seven others. Scores of labor demonstrators were arrested; seven were indicted for murder. The Knights of Labor fell into an immediate decline. The general populace was shocked, angered, and frightened by the Haymarket riots. Church people joined the general populace in arguing that labor organization was "against the law of God." During the next several decades the leaders of the social gospel spoke vigorously for the workers, but they had little influence on rank-and-file church members. They were not well known by slum-dwellers and labor. At best, they constituted "a movement of argument and agitation." [24]

Dissent and violence continued to characterize the labor movement from the 1880s through the 1930s, as the American

Federation of Labor and the Congress of Industrial Organization gave labor the "clout" which the Knights had failed to provide.[25] The Franklin Roosevelt administration fostered legislation which protected labor, and union membership expanded by 300 percent. Sydney Hillman, urging labor to support Roosevelt in 1936, reminded them: "We have participated in making the labor policy of this Administration." [26] In 1937 alone, there were more than 4,700 strikes involving two million workers.

Churchmen ceased to argue that labor organization is "against the law of God," but they united with other middle-class citizens to argue insensitively that it hurt the commonweal. In 1948 the Taft-Hartley Act slowed the pendulum's swing in labor's favor. The strike as an instrument of dissent, however, continued to be a costly weapon in labor-industrial relations. Meanwhile, the corporations, escaping serious public criticism, grew so rapidly—in spite of anti-trust laws on the books—that the giant among them, General Motors, in 1970 controlled larger economic resources than the combined economic resources of a half-dozen major states in the nation. At the close of the 1950s John Kenneth Galbraith, Harvard economist, called for a new social contract between business and society.[27] But little came of his reasoned plea except palaver from the public relations departments of the corporations. The number of "little" stockholders grew enormously. Meanwhile, industry and labor continued to hassle with one another; corporate profits ballooned; the affluent became more affluent; the poor got poorer; and the middle class grew restless over the declining value of their dollar. By 1972 postal workers, schoolteachers, students, policemen, public transportation employees, garbage collectors, and firemen were employing the strike as a weapon to keep their economic heads above water and to preserve their dignity as persons. Major cities were immobilized on occasion. The Labor Department announced in January, 1971, that more man-hours had been lost through strikes in 1970 than in any other year in the preceding decade. The dissent that had been a strand in the life of the American working class since the Jackson revolution had reached a new peak.

To get perspective on 1972, we need to go back to 1890, when the Populists had gained enough strength to establish disturbing battle lines between the corporate giants and the farmers. They were able to make the election of 1896, for the first time since the Civil War, a spirited contest along class lines. On the one side was William McKinley heading the business interests who were convinced that they could govern the country best. On the other side was the liberal wing of the Democrats who had appropriated most of the Populists' objectives—and attracted many Populists—under the leadership of the youthful William Jennings Bryan, the "boy orator from the Platte," who had captured the support of the Democratic Convention with his Cross of Gold speech: "You shall not press down upon the brow of labor this crown of thorns, you shall not crucify mankind upon a cross of gold." [28] Bryan, introducing that famous speech, is reminiscent of progressive leaders in the 1970s: "I come to speak to you in defense of a cause as holy as the cause of liberty—the cause of humanity." [29] The country had not experienced a campaign of such vigor or been subjected to such fanaticism since Jackson swept into office in 1828; and it would not experience another like it until the campaigns of 1928 and 1964. But Bryan was not a radical who planned to reorder society; he was an evangelical humanitarian bent on accomplishing political reforms, curbing class privilege, representing labor and the farmers, and bidding for the support of the lower middle class of his day.

The election of 1896 allied a major political party, the Democrats, with the vigorous attackers of status quo government under Republican leadership. The campaign was vicious. Democrats were charged with anarchism and sedition. Employees were ordered to vote for McKinley or be fired. Their fears were fed by the prospect of receiving wages in depreciated dollars or by wage slashes and unemployment. On Wall Street there was even talk of an Eastern secession if Bryan should win.[30] But big business triumphed; William McKinley was elected. Nonetheless, Bryan had struck fear in the hearts of the ruling class. The Progressive Era was soon to be born. In historical perspective we recognize that Bryan led the last protest of Jefferson's agrarian America against an entrenched industrialism; he also attempted—as Andrew Jackson had done successfully and as Franklin Roosevelt would do in the 1930s—to clean house in American political society. That is what a disorganized but strong-minded, concerned minority seeks to do in the 1970s. They demand a reordering not only of American politics but of society's priorities. Whether a major third party will emerge from these dissidents during the decade is conjectural.

There is an ebb and flow to dissent and violence in American history.[31] The high-water marks have been the American Revolution, the triumph of Jacksonian democracy, the American Civil War, the quest for social justice (1890-1914), the recovery of national purpose in the 1930s, and the triple dissent of the 60s (civil rights, peace, poverty). The lines of contemporary protest are examined in the remainder of this chapter.

Contemporary Dissent

The Vietnam war has brought conscientious objection into the public arena. Previously, the populace had identified this stance with several minor sects. Suddenly it came into public view, especially that aspect called *selective* conscientious objection which rests on "a potentially explosive principle." Selective conscientious objection makes new demands on religious communities that recognize that at times the use of police and military force is necessary, for every use of force must be weighed on its own merits. Equally, it places new demands on the political community which must preserve its sovereignty even while it seeks to honor the individual citizen's conscience. Accordingly, the Supreme Court in an eight to one decision ruled against *selective* conscientious objection in early 1971.

The Supreme Court has broadened the base for conscientious objection so that it now rests on the individual's private judgment and not exclusively on his religious commitment. The first conscientious objectors in America, however, based their claim for exemption from military duty on Christian teaching: the Quakers who arrived in 1656; the Mennonites who arrived in 1683; and the Brethren who arrived in 1719. These sects objected to military service on religious grounds. During the seventeenth century they were persecuted in all the colonies, although Pennsylvania did provide a partial haven.[32] They received whippings; several were executed. But the members of these sects were steadfast in their convictions. Because they were responsible citizens in every other respect, they won grudging recognition from the colonial legislatures. "The people of 'tender conscience' tried the patience of their fellow citizens, but communities were generally content to let them stand aside. And Quakers, on their part, adhered strictly to a doctrine of social quietism. Ever God-fearing, law-abiding men and women, hard workers, they were well thought of by their neighbors. Their views on war were known in the community and they claimed indulgence on no other point. They fulfilled all civic obligations —save one." [33]

When the Civil War engulfed America, especially after the conscription acts, many conscientious objectors were caught up in military service which took them out of their local communities where their views were known (and generally accepted) and placed them in locales where conscience was not honored by military officers who themselves had been conscripted. In many camps these pacifists were tortured—pierced by bayonets, hung by the thumbs, beaten, or placed in solitary confinement—for refusing to carry a musket.[34] As late as World War I, when the law defined a place for the conscientious objector, he still received treatment almost as harsh as that meted out to convicted traitors. During World War II enemy prisoners of war received better treatment than American CO's in some localities.

The broader base for conscientious objection (other than on religious grounds) was defined before the Civil War by Henry

David Thoreau in his "Essay on Civil Disobedience." Thoreau argued that a conscientious objector need not be a man of religious commitment; he could be "a secular man moved by social injustice." [35] But it would be a long century before the American government would act on Thoreau's argument, and then only because thousands of young people, many of whom had no church ties, refused military service during the 1960s on grounds of "conscience." A century before the Supreme Court's historic decision was rendered in 1969, *Harper's Weekly* (1862) was facing reality in a pluralistic society:

> The legislature of Rhode Island lately debated the proposition not to exempt Quakers from military duty. . . . The proposition was lost by a heavy majority. Yet the ground of the defense seems to be unsound. To excuse Quakers, as a religious sect, from duties which are imposed upon all other sects, is evidently a very unequal respect for the sects. The only true ground of excuse should be not that the man is a Quaker, but that he is not resistant. . . . Unless, therefore, all persons who conscientiously object to fighting ought to be released from military duty, there is no good reason why any of them should be.[36]

On another occasion Henry David Thoreau, convinced that he should not contribute to his government's participation in the Mexican War in 1846, flatly refused to pay his poll tax. Philosophically, he argued every individual's right to be a person *vis a vis* monolithic government. Declining to pay his tax and spending a night in the Concord jail, Thoreau suggested a new morality in which each citizen, motivated by ethical constraint, can and must act to turn his political

society from a given course which he considers morally re-
pugnant. A century later hundreds of thousands of young
people were employing Thoreau's argument—"a majority of
one"—in protesting the Vietnam war.

Religious commitment, however, continued to be the base
for many objectors' opposition to war. In 1967 Martin Luther
King, Jr., made his famous "Declaration of Independence
from War in Vietnam," in which he argued that "the relationship of this ministry to the making of peace is so obvious that I
sometimes marvel at those who ask me why I'm speaking
against the war. Could it be that they do not know that the
good news was meant for all men—for communist and cap-
italist, for their children and ours, for black and white, revolutionary and conservative? Have they forgotten that my
ministry is in obedience to the One who loved His enemies so
fully that He died for them? What then can I say to the Viet
Cong or to Castro or to Mao as a faithful minister of this
One? Can I threaten them with death, or must I not share
with them my life." [37] Tragically, Dr. King was required to
sacrifice his life on the balcony of the Lorraine Motel in the
American city of Memphis.

Theoretically and practically, it is democracy's argument
that its political forms and processes minimize the citizen's
need to resort to violence. As long as the state allows dissent,
and responds to it at some points, that claim is substantially
true. However, given the Vietnam war, we must examine the
authenticity of this philosophical claim in present-day American society. Since violence is employed by the sovereign
nation-state in self-defense, and since it is employed by individuals and groups in overcoming social and economic ex-

ploitation of people, a critical examination of the Vietnam war reveals the confusion of millions of American citizens about the place, let alone the right, of dissent in our democratic society. Initially, the American nation-state argued that the Vietnam war was (a) defensive (contain Communism) and (b) liberating (protect South Vietnam against North Vietnam). But as early as the administration of John Kennedy, some dissenters had branded the war an imperialist and exploitative venture. In time millions came to view it as "an American Tragedy in which the United States was itself guilty of war crimes for which it tried the Nazi leadership at Nuremberg a quarter century ago." [38] After a half decade of rising protest in America and harsh criticism from Europe, a new national administration announced—with reluctance and without admission of guilt—that it intended to end the war.

The protest over the war in Indochina has firm precedents in American history: the vigorous reaction against the American Revolution by the Loyalists, against the Mexican war by morally sensitive citizens, against the Civil War by a small minority in the South and a substantial minority in the North, and against the Spanish-American War by those who resisted "yellow journalism." A degree of dissent during any war is a foregone conclusion in any political society, but it is to be expected especially in a democratic state. The Nazi state itself had dissenters. Presently the majority of American citizens agree that some wars have been necessary and may be again in the future. They argue that the state would cease to exist if its citizens were wholly free to decide when and how, if at all, they would participate in war.

But objection to all wars is precisely what a small but growing minority advocate in this nuclear age. Because they are not saying simplistically, as the majority aver, "Better Red than dead," we shall cite examples of their protests and examine their arguments.

Mulford Q. Sibley, professor of political science at the University of Minnesota, has observed that nonviolent resistance took many forms in the 1950s.

> There were vigils before the White House and the Prime Minister's residence in London. The Committee for Nuclear Disarmament in Britain sponsored gigantic marches and demonstrations. . . . Numbers of people in the United States refused to pay income taxes, or at least the portion of their tax that presumably would be used for military defense.
>
> Outright civil disobedience was also employed. Men and women defied New York law by deliberately refusing to take cover during the annual Civil Defense Air Raid Drills, protesting both the futility of civil defense and its role in making people war-minded. Many were arrested and fined or jailed.[39]

A particularly dramatic kind of nonviolent action against preparation for war was the effort to sail ships into the ocean areas where the American government was testing nuclear weapons; a half dozen attempts were made in the late 1950s and early 60s. Typical was the experience of Albert Bigelow, a navy veteran who had become disillusioned with the American military system. He and his four-man crew sailed their ketch, the *Golden Rule,* as far as Honolulu before the United States government obtained a Federal District Court order restraining them from sailing into the Pacific testing area.

Their defiance of that order led to brief jail sentences and probation.[40]

In 1959 Albert Bigelow wrote of his experience under the disquieting title, *The Voyage of the Golden Rule: An Experiment with Truth*.[41] He argued that he and his crew were carrying on a revered American tradition: "Civil disobedience should properly be called *considerate* disobedience. The word 'civil' in the phrase, means with civility, politeness, courtesy, or consideration. It is disobedience with loving-kindness. It is a deliberate act—undertaken after careful and prayerful deliberation. It is never mere revolt against authority. The only unusual thing about considerate disobedience is that Americans should think it unusual. We have a tradition of disobedience." [42]

Nonviolent protests were also carried on at Newport News, Virginia, and New London, Connecticut, against the Government's Polaris submarines.[43] Particularly dramatic was the 1961 peace walk from San Francisco to Moscow. When this committed band of dissenters reached the University of Moscow, efforts were made by the authorities there to halt their scheduled meeting, but Russian students insisted on hearing the dissenters. A meeting of several hours resulted. On October 7, 1961, the tough-minded *Manchester Guardian* commented: "This is far from a trivial happening. In a dictatorship any public outbreak of forbidden ideas is significant; it becomes widely known even if nothing is reported in the press." [44]

A new generation came to adulthood in the decade of the 60s; the change in their attitude was evident. The fight for the ABM missile sites late in the decade was more heavily contested than anyone would have predicted at the height of the cold war. Many young people tackled that issue boldly: "The ABM is an Edsel." The debate over anti-ballistic missiles and retaliatory strength now rages in the halls of government, in homes, in offices, on campuses, in taverns, and on the streets. Dissent from government policies on preparation for nuclear war is decidedly more widespread in the 1970s than it was when President Kennedy took office in 1960. The dissenters have had a measureable impact on the American mind—and the government.

Since mid-1960 the principle of selective conscientious objection has been an issue in American public life. The Universal Military Training and Service Act of the United States allows that a person can be granted legal status as a conscientious objector if he is one "who by reason of religious training and belief, is conscientiously opposed to participation in war in any form." [45] But the Vietnam war produced firm evidence that thousands of young men who did not claim status as conscientious objectors were opposed to the war in Vietnam. What would they do? To whom could they turn? The National Selective Service Act declares that "anyone who knowingly counsels, aids, or abets another to refuse or evade registration or service in the armed forces . . . shall be liable to imprisonment to not more than five years or a fine of $10,000 or both." [46] In the face of that decree, Martin Luther King, Jr., advocated publicly that "every young man who believes this war [Vietnam] is abominable and unjust should file as a conscientious objector." The United Presbyterian Church, the American Baptist Convention, the Lutheran Church in America, the United Church of Christ, the Synagogue Council of

America, and other ecclesiastical bodies pledged their support to selective conscientious objectors. In March, 1971, the United States Supreme Court declared that selective conscientious objection is unconstitutional. Only the person who is opposed on grounds of conscience to *all* wars is legally exempt from military service. The climate of popular opinion in the 70s is notably different from that which prevailed in the 1950s. The American tradition of dissent had escalated throughout the 1960s. A segment of American youth, blacks, liberals, many churchmen, and blocs of politicians have spoken out vigorously against the war in Vietnam, conscription, missile sites, and the arms race. Naturally, these protests evoked counterprotest. "The Establishment reacted by severe repression, by threats, by imprisonment, and by hurling epithets like 'irresponsible' and 'unpatriotic.' Forgetting the long history of dissent, the defenders of the status quo seem to suggest that deliberate disobedience of law is a new thing. Actually, civil disobedience, dissent, and conscientious defiance of law are very old in the history of human thought and action; but defenders of the existing order in every age tend to believe that their own period is peculiar in its rejection of what the rulers of mankind think is best for the world." [47]

Confrontations for conscience' sake raise serious questions for the dissenter, the church, and the government. The crucial questions center on obligation, the justification for dissent and for the repression of it, the purpose of disobedience, the methods of disobedience, etc. What can nonviolence accomplish in a society rooted in and oriented to violence? What does a conscientious individual do, and what does the American State do, when Cain kills Abel or a foreign power endangers its

sovereignty? We do not denigrate Mahatma Gandhi by recalling that the freedom of India roots in many complex
sources other than Gandhi's pacifistic stance. We remember
sadly that Gandhi's nonviolent life ended in a violent deed
against his person. One is constrained to ask: Is self-sacrifice
the ultimate weapon in nonviolence? Is this absolute degree of
dedication possible on a broad scale? Who can promise it
himself? Is it *moral* in the social sense? Absolute pacifists
must answer these and related questions even as nonpacifists
must answer for "limited wars" and for the current threat of
a nuclear holocaust.

First, if a nonviolent society were to be achieved, the entire
concept and purpose of the sovereign nation-state would have
to be radically transformed. "One's imaginative powers are
inadequate to describe a world without military bureaucracies,
conscription, bemedaled generals, twenty-one gun salutes, bud-
get dominated by the call to mass violence, and the centraliza-
tion of power engendered in considerable measure by the
war-State." [48] Is it likely that the nature of the state can be
altered so radically in the foreseeable future?

Second, if a nonviolent society were to be achieved, the
present vast disproportions of wealth and power would have
to be reapportioned. It would no longer be possible for General
Motors and other giant corporations to pour their monies into
development and expansion, nor would it be possible for the
thirty-one million stockholders in American corporations to
expect large profits. Will the corportion management and the
investors pour their monies into poverty programs, etc.? Will
the American people reduce drastically their standard of living
and share their resources liberally to equalize the standard of

living across the world? That seems unlikely on a broad scale.

Third, if a nonviolent society were to be achieved, it would be necessary to create media for conflict management among human beings who differ sharply. The labor mediation board, for example, would have to be pressed a hundred and eighty degrees further and similar media established for reconciliation in warring families, alienated communities, etc. That is a tall order.

Fourth, these three sweeping socio-economic changes could occur only if a radical change in human nature were accomplished. Each human being would have to be able to respect himself as a person. Violence and tyranny exist wherever people have a poor view of themselves and of other human beings. The church, seeking to accomplish the redemption of humanity has converted comparatively few people in nineteen hundred years. The notion that Christianity (or any political ideology) can create an entire society so emotionally and intellectually healthy implies that the Kingdom of God can come inside history. The Christian seeks to create the good (relative) society for the sake of the Kingdom of God. Neither is there any evidence that this herculean task can be accomplished by the Marx-Lenin ideology, the democratic ideology, or any other ideology.

There are biblical bases for man to hope and work and wait for the day when swords are beaten into plowshares, atomic energy is used only for humane purposes, the responsible care of the earth allows people to live comfortably in plenty and peace and beauty. However harassed the peacemakers are, their argument that violence breeds violence is ultimately sound. They provide direction and purpose to less committed mortals. The grim reality is that the nuclear arms race must be controlled; sovereign nation-states must learn to coexist, however uneasily, in a world community of nations; concerned peoples and nations must adjust, to some degree at least, the awesome disparity in living situations. The pacifists point the way in challenging nonpacifists to question whether their position in a particular use of force is historically necessary. Pragmatists can move in the direction they point. It is not ordained that the world must end with a bang or a whimper—in a holocaust or in exhaustion. A series of rational or irrational human decisions will decide that fateful issue one way or the other.

The mood in America is changing. The citizenry recognize the need to update foreign policy so that it is based on contemporary realities rather than archaic assumptions. In 1970 the first new journal on foreign relations in almost fifty years was launched on the premise that the United States requires fresh thinking in this area of its experience if it is to escape catastrophe. The journal *Foreign Policy* aims to challenge the conventional wisdom of hawks and doves, of globalists and isolationists. Writing in the first issue on "Security or Confrontation: The Case for a Defense Policy," Paul C. Warnke and Leslie H. Gelb argue that "the principal lesson of the past decade [1960s] is that military force is a singularly inept instrument of foreign policy and that its use must be limited to direct military threats to American security. Except in such cases, influence and prestige are not served by independent exercise of our military power." [49] In the same issue John Kenneth Galbraith writes: "In the Cuban missile crisis President Kennedy had to balance the danger of blowing up the planet against the risk of political attack at home for appeasing the Communists. This was not an irresponsible choice: to ignore the domestic opposition was to risk losing initiative or office to men who wanted an even more dangerous policy. But there is something more than a little wrong with a system that poses a choice between survival and domestic political compulsion. The missile crisis did not show the strength of our policy; it showed the catastrophic visions and pressures to which it was subject. We were in luck, but success in a lottery is no argument for lotteries." [50] Graham P. Allison, in another article in the new journal, observes that "differences between younger and older Americans are perhaps sharpest when one considers what is likely to be a major issue in American foreign policy for the rest of the century: noninvolvement *vs.* involvement. Whatever their parents may think, young Americans are not 'isolationist' in the sense of wanting to return to the policies of the 1930s; culture and communication and nuclear weapons have laid that ghost to rest. The real debate . . . is over the *extent* of United States military and political involvements overseas." [51]

This new mood of dissent is not only abroad in the university community but also among noncollege youth, too.[52] But it flourished first on college campuses where tomorrow's leaders began experimenting with politics and piety. Tensions mounted; conflicts erupted; the general citizenry was shocked. Of course, there has been tension and conflict between town and gown since the Middle Ages. Several colonial colleges experienced such severe disturbances on occasion that they closed their doors. But during the 1960s campus unrest, student dissent and rebellion was so widespread that it became a national concern. It had begun innocently enough when the Court of Appeals for the Second Circuit of New York decided on September 22, 1959, in the case of *Steier vs. New York State Education Commissioner* that Steier's constitutional rights had not been violated by the college which had expelled him.

Arthur Steier, who was a student at Brooklyn College, argued that the college was dominating student organizations. He presented his views in two critical letters to the president of Brooklyn College. Steier was suspended under a vague rule requiring students to "conform to the requirements of good manners and good morals." Six months later Mr. Steier was readmitted on probation when he agreed to abide by the college rules. But Steier was a convinced dissident; he published the story of his probation in the college newspaper. Again the school expelled him. Mr. Steier judged that his constitutional rights had been violated. The court disagreed; it still viewed attendance at any college or university as a "privilege." Consequently, students could be expelled for any reason which the institution defined and under any procedure which the school authorities considered proper. That longtime view was destined to change.

Early in 1960 students at Alabama State College for Negroes conducted a sit-in after they had been refused service in the lunchroom of the County Courthouse in Montgomery, Alabama. They also participated in mass marches, hymn singing, and speech-making from the steps of the State Capitol. On March 4, 1960, nine students were expelled from the college; twenty were placed on probation. The disciplined students had received no hearing. They had not been advised specifically why they were disciplined. They challenged the action in the court. Like Mr. Steier they were unsuccessful in the Federal District Court, which judged that their constitutional rights had not been violated. The case went to the Court of Appeals for the Fifth Circuit, and on August 4, 1961, the law on the student-university question turned 180 degrees. The decision, *Dixon vs. Alabama State Board of Education,* stated that "whenever a governmental party acts so as to injure an individual, the Constitution requires that the act be consonant with due process of law."

This change in legal interpretation reflects a fundamental change in American student life. Whereas a college education had been regarded for decades as a luxury, it was now viewed as a necessity for millions of high school graduates. Further, it reflected that college students are not children and, therefore, have the right to self-determination. In 1968 Judge James E. Doyle, Western District Court of Wisconsin, declared that there had been "a profound shift in the nature of American schools and colleges and universities, and in the relationships between younger and older people. These changes seldom have been articulated in judicial decisions but they are increasingly reflected there. The facts of life have long since undermined the concepts, such as *in loco parentis,* which have been invoked historically for conferring upon university authorities virtually limitless disciplinary discretion."

Judge Doyle further observed, "I take notice that particularly in recent years the universities have become theaters for stormy and often violent protest over such matters as war and peace, racial discrimination in our cities and elsewhere, and the quality of American life; that this phenomenon adds new and unanticipated dimensions to the regulation of conduct in the university; and that those charged with governments of these institutions have been struggling to preserve the many competing values involved." [53] So the Constitution came to the campus of the state university. It is not likely that private colleges and universities will provide fewer rights for their students than those granted to students being educated in state institutions. Nonetheless, harsh exceptions in both state and private schools continue to persist.

The 1970 tragedies at Kent State University and Jackson State are burned into the public mind. Yet the local courts in Ohio and Mississippi evidenced little regard for the rights of those students as citizens. On October 15, 1970, indictments were returned against twenty-four students and one faculty member of Kent State University by a special grand jury in Portage County, Ohio. The indictments were contrary to the findings of other investigative parties which had looked into the tragic events that occurred on the Kent State campus May 4, 1970, including the Federal Bureau of Investigation and the President's Commission on Campus Unrest. Further, a prosecuting attorney who presented the Kent State cases to the grand jury was later quoted as having said after the indictments were released that the National Guardsmen should have shot all the troublemakers. Another example of the grand jury's prejudices and high-handedness was the "gag" order issued by the judge who had convened it, which forbade any public criticism of its proceedings by any participant. Except for the indictments, that grand jury report was later withdrawn and ordered destroyed by judicial decision—but the psychic damage had been done.

A few months after the Portage County Court handed down its decision, Judge Millard L. Midonick of the New York Family Court ruled that the father of a hippie daughter in college could *not* cut off her funds because he deplored her life-style. An increasing number of courts are treating young people as adults who have constitutional rights.[54]

We have said little, except implicitly, about racial dissent and violence. That tragedy embedded in American history has been debated since the first boatload of slaves reached America. Little more needs to be added here. Distinct advances in civil rights for blacks have been made under the Johnson and Nixon administrations, but they do not satisfy the American black. Frustrated by two hundred years of being treated as property and another hundred years of being exploited as third-class citizens, the blacks are *raging* against the whites. The black American—ripped from his African home, his past torn from him, a new language and culture pressed upon him—has been dehumanized and exploited by white society. As Chief Justice Roger Taney put it in 1859 in the infamous Dred Scott decision: "A black man has no rights which a white man is bound to respect." That is still true in 1972 in many places. The American church has not helped materially. It has, with notable exceptions, "incorporated into its own life and practices the separatist ways of the society. The doors of the church were either closed to Blacks or the churches held special services for Blacks—or opened their doors to Blacks but segregated them within the churches. The now famous 'nigger balconies' of the churches resulted from this latter practice." [55]

Throughout American history the black people and the

black church have functioned outside white theology.[56] The white majority of the nation, hostile and oppressive, has been aided and abetted by a conspiring or consenting white church.[57] This racism in *all* segments of white society has nurtured a deep rage in most blacks, especially the young. Senator Fred Harris has stated, "When my colleagues and I on the National Advisory Committee on Civil Disorders concluded that the deepest cause of the recent riots in our cities was white racism, we went as directly as we knew how to the heart of the matter. . . . Despite the passage of five civil rights bills since 1957, despite the erosion of legal supports for segregated institutions, despite greater acceptance of Negroes into our major institutions, both public and private, it is still no easy thing to be a black person in America. . . . This is to say that for the average Negro 'so much time has passed and so little has changed.' " [58]

C. T. Vivian, in a concise, hard-hitting paperback, *Black Power and the American Myth,* describes the current sociopolitical situation accurately: "Liberty, equality, and justice are truly parts of our democratic inheritance; but this is an inheritance which we have never fully claimed, for it is inextricably bound to another—the legacy of slavery. This too is a part of America's tradition; and we have been unable to separate one from the other." [59]

Vivian believes that the civil rights movement failed because it rested on the myth that legislation would effect justice. One may argue the relationship between law and justice in other areas of societal experience and win a dialectical argument over Mr. Vivian—as Dr. Eck won a dialectical victory over Dr. Luther at the Leipzig Debate (1519)—yet that does not alter reality: the average black is not yet free to be a person in America, the "land of the free." There is a difference between legislation and justice. The average black knows this in *his own* experience.

Psychiatrists William H. Grier and Price M. Cobbs have written one of the more "important books on the Negro to appear in the last decade." [60] In it they argue poignantly:

> People bear all they can and, if required, bear even more. But if they are black in present-day America, they have been asked to shoulder too much. They have had all they can stand. They will be harried no more. Turning from their tormentors, they are filled with rage. The growing anger of Negroes is frightening to white America. . . . If racist hostility is to subside, and if we are to avoid open conflict on a nationwide scale, information is the most desperately needed commodity of our time. And of the things that need knowing, none is more important than that all blacks are angry. White Americans seem not to recognize it. They seem to think that all the trouble is caused by only a few "extremists." They ought to know better. We have talked to many Negroes under the most intimate of circumstances and we know better.[61]

One recalls the report of the Kerner Commission: "Our nation is moving toward two societies, one black, one white—separate and unequal." [62] That judgment is highlighted in the motion picture *Joe*. The lower middle-class American is frustrated, angry, rebellious. The American ethnic is troubled at what he considers to be the "changing of the rules." He feels he had to suffer humiliation and defeat and to work constantly to achieve the socio-economic situation he presently "enjoys." Now, other groups are demanding these positions as a matter of right. He argues angrily that the American ethnics'

> children had to pass entrance exams to get into college; other men's children (they think) do not. *Their* fathers had to work long hours to support their families; other men's fathers seemingly did not. *They* fought bravely to defend America in World War II and in the Korean War, and now it is being alleged that those who fight and die in wars are immoral or foolish. *They* lived according to the American ethic of sobriety and respectability, and now they see on TV the spectacle of the drug-smoking hippie at a rock festival. In other words, the white ethnic feels that he is being told that the rules no longer apply, that others are to achieve what he has achieved (frequently, it seems to him, with his picking up the tab) by doing exactly the opposite of what the rules prescribed. There is obviously something incomplete, perhaps something paranoic, about this "change of rules" analysis. But Mr. Agnew's success is the mark of the plausibility it enjoys. He who wishes to make converts to the cause of peace among those who think the rules are changing has his work cut out for him.[63]

Who seeks to make converts to the cause of peace does indeed have his work cut out for him. The blue-collar citizen has borne the brunt of America's quest for racial justice during the last decade. Generally speaking, it is *his* children's school that is threatened by desegragation, it is *his* job which is in jeopardy when blacks are employed, and, most burdensome, it is *his* neighborhood which is pushed to accept black and other disadvantaged residents. Suburbia, the seat of Protestantism (and increasingly of Catholicism), mouths pious platitudes while expecting "Joe" to make democracy work.[64] That has been happening for decades. Now, "Joe," weary of bearing the brunt of racial change, is rebelling. The current fragmentation of American society requires creative, cohesive leadership at all levels of government, church, and school. That leadership has not emerged.

The renaissance of a venerable band of dissenters in American history also deserves inclusion here: the feminist leaders. This movement is subjected in some quarters to wholesome humor and in others to ridicule. Joan Baez, for example, who has made a career of crusading for peace, civil rights, and ecology—everything except Women's Liberation—is reported to have said in 1970: "I can't take it [Lib] seriously. I mean, if I'm carrying my guitar and my baby, and my husband's in jail, I'm not going to yell at some guy who holds the door open for me." [65] But Women's Liberation is not essentially concerned with that, or "bra burning," or clothes styles, or career *vs.* marriage, or free love. These are peripheral issues in the movement.

Basically, Women's Liberation attacks the social, economic, political, and religious practices (consciously and unconsciously subscribed) which require or coerce the female to be less than a whole person. Significantly, the movement is not a contemporary phenomenon inspired and goaded by the dissent of youth and blacks. It has deep, honorable antecedents in American history. The nineteenth-century secular reformers of New England and the Middle West, many of them Quakers and Unitarians, made sweeping attacks on the grievous faults in

American society. Women constituted a *majority* in both these reforming groups. "If there is any reliable generalization to be made about the 'female character' it is that it is on the whole more responsive to suffering and inhumanity than its masculine counterpart. Women . . . had always been better represented in the religious life of the communities. . . . They were in a majority in the reform movements which began to burgeon by the end of the eighteenth century. . . . The most important involvement of American women in the years between the American Revolution and the outbreak of the Civil War was in the anti-slavery movement. The woman's rights movement was an offshoot of the agitation against slavery." [66] These names loom large in American history: Nette Blackwell, Lucy Stone, Harriet Beecher Stowe, Susan B. Anthony, Elizabeth Cady Stanton. Suffrage reform (accomplished in 1919) was carried along on "the momentum generated by the little band of reformers who had taken up the cause in the two decades preceding the Civil War." [67] Taking a firm place in the anti-slavery movement, women shared the leadership of a significant social movement for the first time in history.[68] Thereafter, they pursued a larger place for themselves in American society.

Allowing for a measure of exaggeration and a hint of self-righteousness, there is substantial truth in this nineteenth-century *History of Woman Suffrage:* "Women," the editor opined, "had been victims of the 'same principle of selfishness and love of power in man that has thus far dominated weaker nations and classes.' This impulse to domination was encouraged by 'the slavish instinct of an oppressed class. . . . She has long been bought and sold, caressed and crucified at the will and pleasure of her master.' " [69]

The history of Women's Liberation is long and honorable in American history, but its history is older—as old as Christianity itself. Leonard Swidler, a member of the religion department at Temple University, has argued recently on clear biblical and theological grounds that "Jesus was a feminist." [70] Jesus clearly taught that the female is a human being entitled to all the rights and privileges attendant to personhood. Dissent and protest are essential in an American society which does not yet accord her those rights and privileges.

* * * * *

Dissent has surged through American life from 1607 to 1972. Frequently violence occurred, and most frequently it was employed deliberately *against* dissenters to *preserve* the socioeconomic status quo. But during the 1960s the tables were turned; the dissidents employed violence. A new chapter in the life of the church emerged.

Chapter 5

THE CHURCH AND THE STATE

*To Wesley a scheme to reconstruct society which ignored
the redemption of the individual was unthinkable, but a
doctrine to save sinning men, with no aim to transform them
into crusaders against social sin was equally unthinkable.*
                                                    —Henry Carter

Since we shall attempt in this chapter to define more specifically how piety and politics intermingle in American society, it is necessary to sketch the classical views on Christ and culture, discern more sharply the essential nature and purpose of church and state, and outline several ways in which Christians (and the church) relate to the state.

Christ and Culture

One classic view places culture above Christ.[1] That was the inflexible position of Imperial Rome: "Hail Caesar, we who are about to die salute you." The only authentic charge brought against Jesus before Pilate was that he honored God above the Roman Emperor (the state). If Pilate had released Jesus, he would not have been "Caesar's friend." This view—state over church—has persisted across the centuries. Henry VIII appealed to it. The Spanish sovereigns reveled in it. Mussolini maneuvered his Fascist party into a position of power over the Roman Catholic Church in twentieth-century Italy. The Nazi state domesticated the Christian Church in Germany except for a remnant.[2] Soviet Russia and her satellite states have accomplished the same feat.

Joseph Hromádka's heartbroken letter to the Kremlin after the Soviets' purge of Czechoslovakia's liberal political leadership in 1968 puts the conflict in clear focus: the totalitarian state must be dominant over all other social institutions.[3] No totalitarian state can or will tolerate *any* social institution which is effectively critical of its political theory or public policies. Repression or domestication always occurs. The statement of this reality is not equivalent to endorsing the political rightists' uncritical assumption that Communists are behind every door in the government, church, and university in the United States, or that every Communist state is a rigid monolithic structure.

Millions of comfortable Americans who criticize the Communists' oppressive measures against dissenting churchmen, educators, editors, scientists, poets, and novelists actually suppress and repress dissent in America by supporting socially biased newspapers, fostering public education which is subservient to political pressures, endorsing a government which clings neurotically to the status quo, and criticizing a church which demonstrates active concern for persons-in-society. Many American church members honor the state above the

127

church in their uncritical endorsement of sectional political goals and chauvinistic interests of the state. Some admit to this; others deny it vociferously. Only small segments of society acknowledge Christ as the Lord of the church and fewer still acknowledge him as Lord of any social institution in American society in 1972.[4] Cultural accommodation is a vigorous strand in American Christianity. Consequently, when churchmen like King, Groppi, the Berrigans, and Stringfellow come on the scene, conflict is inevitable.

Another view on Christ and culture presents the opposite end of the spectrum—Christ above culture. Beginning with the first generation of Christians, this view has had dedicated supporters. It contends that Christ is outside of, above, and unconcerned about culture; that God is interested only in man's "spiritual life"; that public issues lie outside Christian concern. Firm evidences of this view persist in contemporary society. Religious monasticism and sectarianism have a host of "kissin' cousins" outside ecclesiastical circles: "ivory tower" professors, "pure" scientists, "secular" political leaders, and Bob Dylan's "private" salvation (currently, one segment of young people has retreated into privatism, seeking to escape worldly pressures and ignoring the ambiguities of contemporary history). Andrew Hacker contends that privatism has become *the* pervasive reality in American society (a nation of "two hundred million egos"). He considers this a threat to the preeminence and possibly the existence of the American nation.[5]

Sectarian Protestantism is yet another evidence of the Christ above culture concept. During the seventeenth century bands of committed Christians, persecuted in and impoverished by the religious wars in Europe, established communal life apart from the "evil" society which persecuted them. Three centuries later, many sectarians in America are living in social isolation because they orient to these "dated emotions." [6] The interaction of Christ and culture is reality; God has acted and continues to act in his world. Specifically, sectarianism does not liberate its adherents from basic political responsibilities in the sovereign American state: taxes must be paid; military exemption is a privilege rather than a right; traffic laws must be obeyed; etc.

The view that Christ is unrelated to culture is not limited, however, to monastics and sectarians. It is subscribed to by millions of main-line Protestant, Catholic, and Orthodox churchmen in America who view religion wholly as a private affair. In practice they share corresponding viewpoints with the advocates of the secular state. But biblical Christianity calls the church to bring both private and public life under the judgment and mercy of God's Word for the sake of a humane society. That is an inescapable implication of the Incarnation. Jesus was not a disembodied spirit. He lived in the world under the legal jurisdiction of Rome; "he suffered under Pontius Pilate," a Roman governor, and was crucified by the state. [7]

A third view of Christ and culture is syncretistic. It calls for the gospel and culture to be a meld. Many scholars judge that such a meld occurred absolutely during the high Middle Ages—the Age of Faith. Others disagree, but the reality is that the syncretistic concept reached a high level during the thirteenth century when Thomas Aquinas was *the* influential mind in Western thought. Rational reductions were made in the ethic of Jesus; meanwhile, the secular ethic was upgraded.

We have also seen how syncretism is a strand in the history of American Christianity.[8] American nationalism and a vigorous though shallow evangelicalism fused during the nineteenth century to form religion-in-general and to contribute to a civic piety. Of course, Christian syncretism is not a phenomenon of the thirteenth century in western Europe or the nineteenth century in America; it has a long history. In the eighth century B.C. the Hebrew prophets—Amos, Isaiah, Hosea, and Micah—attacked it relentlessly. Jesus identified its dangers. Paul argued against it. John rejected it.

A fourth view contends that Christianity and culture exist in tension: the Christian decides personal and social issues for himself in the light of Christ's mind and pays the price for the position he elects to honor. Essentially, this was Paul's view. He exhorted the little bands of Christians to honor the state so long as that was possible without letting the world squeeze them into its mold. Oscar Cullmann argues that if the early Christians had not been ordered to worship the Emperor, the book of Revelation would not have been written. The Roman state's claim of supremacy over God prodded the early church to charge the state with overstepping its God-ordained responsibility to provide order and justice. Cullmann demonstrates that this same view is implied in Paul's writings on the state. We concur in that judgment. Augustine and Luther in turn took over this view of two realms under God and fashioned it into "the doctrine of the two kingoms." [9] Handled flexibly, related dynamically to modern society, and formulated in today's idiom, the doctrine provides clues for living responsibly under the gospel in the sovereign democratic nation-state which, while concerned with order and justice, is jealous of its own sovereignty.[10]

Biblical Christianity—rejecting monasticism, sectarianism, and syncretism—provides the ground for the development of the doctrine of the two kingdoms: Christ and culture in tension, church and state in polarity, piety and politics in dynamic relationship. The Christian citizen has obligations to *both* church and state. His ultimate allegiance, however, belongs to *neither* institution; it belongs to God. Every Christian is obliged to honor God's claim on his conscience which, acted on, may or may not alter the course of the state (Bonhoeffer failed) or the direction of the ecclesiastical church (Luther succeeded partially). In all seasons the church's impact on the state is both indirect and direct. The direct impact is accomplished through the elective processes (in a democratic state) and through dissent from and resistance to any state policies which dehumanize society.[11]

Thomas Jefferson, brooding over the reenactment of the religious persecutions of Europe on American shores, fostered the Statute of Religious Freedom in Virginia. When the Constitution was up for ratification, he encouraged his "Republican" colleagues to demand an amendment to the federal Constitution which would provide for separation of church and state as free institutions in society. Jefferson feared clericalism in an established church, but it never occurred to him that churchmen-citizens would decline to speak out on political, economic, and social issues which concerned them. That right, after all, was guaranteed by the First Amendment. His view prevailed in the nineteenth century. The American state was neutral toward religious traditions, declined to interfere directly with the many churches and sects, yet did not choose to be wholly secular in its attitude toward its citizens' religious life or their judgment of the relevance of their religious views to affairs of state. It is in this context that Henry Steele Commager could identify the nation at the opening of the twentieth century as "a Christian nation" in everything but law.[12]

The fact that Jefferson was a deist, Paine an agnostic, Washington an Episcopalian, and Adams a Congregationalist disturbs Christian purists; they fear a civic piety which can obscure the distinct Christian traditions. The several churches, indifferent toward their confessional positions, are responsible for that phenomenon. The church in America is *legally* free to be true to the gospel.[13]

A large segment of contemporary American church members are less knowledgeable and concerned about their political and biblical traditions than their eighteenth- and nineteenth-century forebears were. Actively or passively, the Christian's attitudes toward politics and economics—and all social issues —reflect his emotional and intellectual commitment to Christ —or lack of it. Christians are citizens. The sectarian who argues that the church should "preach Christ" and stay out of politics becomes politically active over "religious" issues which concern him. The Amishman, for example, goes to court when his views on the education of his young are threatened by the state. Conscientious objection is a political issue as well as a religious and moral issue. Because people are human (it depends on whose ox is being gored) the constitutional separation of church and state is ingenious. It guarantees legally that the state cannot dictate what the church's witness shall be. Equally, it guarantees legally that a sect or denomination or a wider segment of Christendom cannot dictate that the state shall legislate in favor of that particular sect or denomination or segment of Christendom. The influence of the Roman Catholic Church in blocking the dissemination of birth control information in Massachusetts and Connecticut during the 1950s and 1960s was a violation of the separation of church and state. Equally, Bible reading in the public schools was a violation of the First Amendment. Jefferson and his contemporaries would be distressed by the political naïveté and casuistry of many contemporary churchmen and by the rigid secular prejudice of many unchurched citizens who argue jointly that the church should be disallowed from speaking on political issues. That would disenfranchise half the citizenry. Further, the church, if it is true to the Word of God, is constrained to speak concretely on all human issues: war, poverty, racism, ecology, etc. Whenever the church declines to speak on these and other human concerns, it denies the Incarnation (God so loved the world) and the Resurrection (Christus Victor is Lord). In America any declination of this responsibility reveals the church to be an irresponsible corporate citizen.

Interaction between the institutions of church and state is inevitable because (a) Christ redeems human life; (b) Christians are citizens of the state; (c) politics is a means of establishing order and promoting justice among peoples; (d) the Constitution guarantees freedom of religion, speech, press, and assembly. The formal separation of the institutions of church and state safeguards society against secular-minded citizens and/or church-oriented citizens who would seek to enact coercive measures through *either* institution. In countries where a state church has existed or exists presently, religious minorities were or are discriminated against: Huguenots in France, Anabaptists in Germany, the Puritans in England, Hindus and Moslems in India and Pakistan, Buddhists in Vietnam, etc. Spain and Latin America have been severely maimed by ecclesiastical coercion in their political life. Presently Catholicism is struggling to exercise a prophetic role in Latin America. If it succeeds, political and religious polarization will become more acute in the southern hemisphere, especially in Brazil. On the other hand, if the church fails and slips into yesteryear's state-church style, Catholicism may die in Latin America.[14] The cleavage between Catholic, Protestant, and Orthodox churches and the American democratic state is not nearly so severe, but it is deepening; politics and piety are in conflict. The human constituencies of both institutions are, after all, the same people in at least half the cases. Interaction is inevitable.

Our cursory survey of American history has revealed that churchmen—especially in the eighteenth and nineteenth centuries—joined actively with nonchurchmen to build the American political society on the foundations of Britain's Atlantic community. Both reacted consciously and unconsciously to classic Judeo-Christian teachings, an emerging folk religion, Lockean principles, a growing "civic piety," and the sociopsychological impact of immigration and the frontier.[15] The current flight from political responsibility in some quarters of the church is not only unbiblical but also contrary to the letter and the spirit of the Constitution. Practical politics and Christian piety interact; they cannot be compartmentalized. Our forebears recognized, accepted, and demonstrated that reality.

The Nature and Purpose of the Church and the State

What is the nature and purpose of the church? That question brings us face to face with divergent doctrines and folk concepts of the church. Full agreement among Christians on the nature and purpose of the church is not possible. It is possible, however, to set down concisely from the biblical sources what the majority of Christians can and do agree on concerning the nature and purpose of the church.

(1) The church is a divine-human community which exists to testify to the mighty deeds of God in human history. A substantial bloc of main-line Protestants and Catholics agree that the Living Word comes to man through myth, legend, drama, historical events, persons—and fully in the historical person of Jesus of Nazareth as presented in the Bible.[16] They may not agree on the methodology of discerning the Word of God in the words of men, but they do agree that the church is a divine-human community entrusted with the Word of God.

(2) The church reflects God's intention. Christians agree that "the church is not an accidental, secondary element in the Christian Faith—as if God had really willed to save individuals, who through misguided gregarious instinct and evil power-impulses mistakenly formed for themselves a community of worship. Rather . . . the church . . . is a fundamental part of the divine purpose, willed by God and established by him just as much as the Incarnation itself. . . . The church, therefore, is a vital part of the gospel itself." [17] The argument that Jesus did not establish an "ecclesia" disintegrates when it is hailed before the tribunal of biblical evidence. Scripture

testifies that Jesus *called* twelve disciples, *instructed* them intensively, and *sent* them into the world to carry on what he had initiated. The argument (based on Harnack's view) that the church was established by Jesus' first-century followers, who in turn corrupted the purity of his message, is refuted by the bulk of critical studies. Biblical scholarship traces a clear line from Jesus and his disciples through the primitive church in Jerusalem to the churches of Paul and John, Barnabas and Luke.

Scripture provides four arguments that Jesus fashioned a new Israel, a church. (a) The Kingdom of God, at the heart of Jesus' words and works, implies the gathering of a community. (b) The idea of messiahship, as Jesus interpreted it, implies the calling together of a *new* people of God. (c) When Jesus spoke of himself as doing a shepherd's work, he was describing his messianic task of gathering the people of God. This is a continuing event. (d) Jesus called twelve disciples, taught them, sent them, empowered them, instituted a covenant with them, which reveals him deliberately executing his messianic task of creating a new Israel, the people of God.[18]

(3) Christians agree that the Christian Church, from the beginning, fashioned evangelical forms to (a) persuade persons to embrace Christ and to care for them in its community, (b) preserve and defend apostolic truth, and (c) carry the promises and demands of Christ into the world. How these tasks are to be executed divides churchmen, but they are in agreement concerning the tasks themselves. Christianity has been able to bridge the centuries by providing a spirit-inhabited institution through which the Word has become flesh in each succeeding generation. The historical Jesus, a

child of his times, did not envision the medieval ecclesiastical hierarchy, the Industrial Revolution, "the garbled lexicon of quantum physics," presidential elections, the cold war, the "cool" medium, or fligths to the moon. His church, however, has lived to experience all these and more. Led by his Spirit, it has shaped historical forms through which Christ himself has confronted persons in time and from within which and through which it could accomplish God's mission in the world. Neither scripture nor Christian history supports the view that one particular pattern of organization or any one form of worship prevailed in the early church or in the church from its origin until now. There are varieties of Christian experience; the Bible bristles with them. There are varieties of liturgical forms; Christian history is crammed with them.[19]

The church is the people of God, created by God, redeemed by Christ, and nurtured by the Holy Spirit. It exists to proclaim the gospel, to instruct and care for persons from that gospel, and to serve persons in the world. During the first three centuries of its existence the church carried on these tasks through illegal assemblies in homes and catacombs, through clandestine dialogues, and through illegal acts in shops, marketplaces, and along the trade routes. Proclamation and instruction persuaded one person, several, or a small assembly (congregation). Preaching and teaching the Word, initiated by Jesus and carried on by his disciples, are functions of the whole church. The tasks can be carried on in as many different ways as there are different persons among the people of God. Individual witness (Bonhoeffer, Berrigan, Groppe Stringfellow) and collective declarations (on the Vietnam war, poverty, racial discrimination) can be equally consistent with the gospel.

The church exists to safeguard apostolic truth. It is the historic task of the church not only to share the apostolic truth but to be its custodian. Friedrich Gogarten has warned that the two most serious threats to the gospel in our day against which it must be protected are its being dissolved into a myth and its being hardened into a religion of law.[20] There are other serious threats to the gospel in American life. America nurtures syncretistic religion: civil piety and religion-in-general blur the particularistic genius of the Reformation and Catholic traditions.[21] Closely allied with syncretistic religion is the "new paganism" which values human experience primarily in terms of the five senses. Another danger exists in the form of thousands of lackluster congregations which present the gospel in forms which obscure the gospel's awful relevancy. Equally dangerous are the "gung-ho parishes" which place apparent relevance above the fundamentals of the Faith.

The church exists to do Christ's commandments. That can happen only in the world through acts of service to persons regardless of their condition, color, or creed. To work for fair housing, equal employment opportunities, and justice in the courts are acts of priestly service. Person-to-person testimony to Christ is not intelligible to *secular* man except through deeds related to his cultural experience. Each congregation must bring persons, mores, ideologies, and institutions under the judgment of God's Word. This responsibility, accepted by persons in concrete situations, produces tension and engenders conflict. This *brand* of conflict is a condition for Christian reconciliation.

"The worship of God," Whitehead observes, "is not a rule of safety." It cost John the Baptist his head. It cost Jesus of Nazareth his life. It cost John a season of exile on the Isle of Patmos. It exposed Paul to beatings, stonings, shipwreck, martyrdom. Christian worshipers march to a different drumbeat, but they march *in the world*. Wesley and his lay preachers ministered in the dirtiest corners of poverty-ridden London in the mid-eighteenth century. Kagawa offered priestly service in the slums of Yokohama. Bishop Dibelius, resisting the Nazis in the early 1930s, was denied his pulpit by Hitler before World War II. Bonhoeffer was hanged for his participation in the bomb plot against the Nazi Fuehrer in 1944. Authentic Christians are deeply involved in the world. Nineteen centuries ago a handful of slaves, merchants, fishermen, Roman soldiers, and women worshiped God in private homes and catacombs; they became so involved in the world that centuries later the classical English historian Edward Gibbon, surprised and angered at discovering their influence, charged them with contributing significantly to the fall of the Roman Empire.[22]

It is in this sense that John Bennett judges that "the most important type of impact of the church on society or the state is indirect." [23] He means that the churches do not set out deliberately to influence economic or political decisions but do in fact influence them through the Christian witness of their members as citizens. In the remainder of this chapter and in chapter 6, we shall consider the indirect and direct ways in which the church influences the state for good and ill.

First, however, it is necessary to enunciate more sharply the nature and purpose of the state. That requires the identification of the classic views of the state in Christian history.

The American democratic state exists to ensure order, promote justice, reflect majority rule, guarantee the right of dissent, and protect its citizens against internal and external aggression. To meet these responsibilities it must maintain its sovereignty. That is accomplished in part by the state's positive responses to the strongest political and economic forces in its constituency. Consequently, dissent from the state's policies may come from the majority (as it did in the Jackson and Roosevelt elections of 1828 and 1932) or from minorities (as it has on the Vietnam war, nuclear testing, etc.).

The state in the time of Jesus and Paul and John and Peter had little in common with the nation-states of North America and western Europe except for the need to preserve its sovereignty. Through the Roman Emperor's deputies the scores of provinces in the Mediterranean world and in western Europe were subjected absolutely to Rome's decrees. Only a Roman citizen could appeal to the Emperor. In some provinces —Judea, Gaul, Britain—the Emperor's deputy (governor) exercised absolute authority in the name of Rome. Consequently, the Pharisees, clamoring for Jesus' crucifixion, could not accomplish their purpose without a direct order from the Roman governor. Pilate maintained peace in his province by authorizing the crucifixion of a man he personally considered to be innocent.[24] The New Testament writers, bent on laying blame on the Pharisees, glossed over the hard reality that the state killed Jesus. The Roman state did not originate the charges against Jesus or press them, but it did accede to the demands of a minority in Judea to keep the peace. The Pharisees did not live politically, as Americans do, under the doctrine of "the consent of the governed"; they had no legal voice in the crucifixion. They were morally guilty; they were legally innocent. The democratic nation-states of the twentieth century have little in common with the Roman Empire of New Testament days.

Nonetheless, Paul argued that all people, including Christians, should honor the authority of the state since it was established by God to ensure order and preserve domestic tranquility (Romans 13). Peter advanced the same argument. John, during a period of religious persecution, branded the Roman state as the anti-Christ (I Peter 2). Oscar Cullmann argues convincingly that there is no contradiction between the views of Paul and John.[25] So long as "rulers are not a terror to good conduct" they are to be obeyed. But if the state attacks persons of good conduct—and especially if, in effect, it demands that all citizens worship its sovereign will (that is, places itself above God)—the Christian must resist the state. Paul implied that principle. Peter was adamant on this point although he was speaking specifically at the time about resisting Jewish religious authorities: "We ought to honor God rather than men." The apostolic faith flourished for three centuries as an illegal religion; it was bootlegged through the Mediterranean world. During its clandestine existence, the church lacked both the numbers and the organization to influence the state *directly*. Consequently, the New Testament literature has little to say specifically on how direct influence is to be accomplished.

Early in the fourth century Constantine staked out a new

historical situation for the church; he granted Christianity not only legal but preferred status. Church membership soared; its institutional forms mushroomed; it became a land-owner; it began to lust after secular power. By the eleventh century the ecclesiastical institution in the West so yearned for worldly power that it tried to bring the state under its domination. Five centuries later the Calvinists, a vigorous band of reformers, executed a similar power-grab in establishing theocratic government in Geneva, Swtizerland. There, the church's vast secular power was demonstrated cruelly when Michael Servetus, a dissenter from Calvinism, was burned at the stake. A century later in colonial New England, the theocratic Puritans sought to define private morality through political legislation. Different types of government reflect different concepts of the state.

The first overarching concept of church and state appears in Augustine's intellectually sophisticated classic *The City of God*. The Bishop of Hippo, convinced of man's depravity, viewed the state as necessary for law, order, and peace. He argued that the church can go about its work only if the state fulfills its God-ordained function. However, both *institutions* —state and church—are described in the *City of Man* as being imperfect, infected by evil, and impermanent.

John Bennett observes that "there is a contrast in Christian thinking about the state between those Christians who regard the state as entirely, or almost entirely, the result of the fall of man, as the divine provision for dealing with the consequences of sin, and those who, while not denying this negative role of the state, emphasize its positive functions as an instrument of human cooperation, as a constructive agency for human welfare that expresses the social nature of man." [26]

Roman Catholic thought inclines to the view that the state as an instrument reflects the social nature of man. The natural law, discernible by human reason, provides the principles for its structure and operation.[27] Rommen, in his *The State in Catholic Thought,* declares that "the state proceeds by inner moral necessity from the social nature of man for the sake of the more perfect life, the fuller realization of personality for all its members in a working sovereign order of mutual assistance and mutual cooperation." [28] Given this view, citizens are less disposed to criticize or dissent from a government's policies, yet the need for criticism and dissent is implicit in the argument.

The Protestant Reformation precipitated a totally different concept of the state. Among the Reformers, Luther's view was the most radical. He was convinced that Providence had ordained the state to prevent anarchy and foster social order. The state was God's agent to overrule and check man's sin. It existed to protect its citizens against aggression, to keep order, and to punish crime. Politics could be a vocation approved by God. But if Luther identified the origin of the state with man's sin, he also recognized that there is a special embodiment of sin in the state itself. He averred that one must "know that from the beginning of the world a wise prince is a rare bird in heaven, still more a pious prince.'" [29] Luther fixed a firm wall between church and state, removing the gospel sharply from the state's province, when he declared that it would be better to have a "wise Turk" at the head of the state than "a foolish Christian." He was convinced that it was not within the province of the church to use the state to achieve the gospel's purposes.

Luther's clean division between the two institutions (which the American Constitution embodies) has had a salutary impact on twentieth-century theology. Reinhold Niebuhr and other Reformation theologians managed a vigorous critique of liberal theology and moral idealism by reasserting Luther's insistence that the state, necessary in maintaining order, is nonetheless "an embodiment of pride and imperialism in relation to other states and a tyrant in relation to its own citizens; that even the relatively good state, in the pursuit of peace and justice, is limited not only by its own sinfulness as a center of power but also by the moral limitations of the people of the nation as a whole in their approach to the needs and the aspirations and the fears of other nations, by the tragic dilemmas which arise in the international sphere in which its responsibility to have the military power to defend its freedom becomes part of the general threat to human existence in a nuclear age, and by the tendencies among ordinary men to lose incentive and to become irresponsible when the state is most effective in improving their conditions." [30]

In sharp contrast, John Calvin argued that the state did not originate because of man's sin but because of God's providence. He viewed the state as an adjunct of the church. The salutary significance of Luther's hard-nosed separation of the two institutions comes into focus when one ponders Calvin's judgment that "civil government is designed, as long as we live in this world, to cherish and support the external worship of God, to preserve the pure doctrine of religion, to defend the constitution of the church." [31] Calvin's view produced the harsh theocratic government in Geneva which authorized the burning of Servetus at the stake. Modified slightly, it produced Cromwell's England with its harsh "religious" restrictions. It also produced the Puritan oligarchy in colonial New England which searched out "witches" and, in the dead of winter, drove Roger Williams into the wilderness because of his religious dissent from the Puritan establishment.

The Calvinist view (and its state church) dominated American colonial life for 150 years, especially in New England. On the other hand, it did fire America's quest for freedom from Britain and prodded the Founding Fathers to fashion a government that was flexible and durable. But following the Revolution, the impact of Calvin's church-state thinking on American society (Puritan theocracy) continued in some states. Although the Constitution's First Amendment called for the separation of church and state, tax-supported churches existed in Connecticut until 1818 and in Massachusetts until 1833. The American Constitution "created a new pattern of church-state relations, unknown since the first century": the system of voluntarism.[32] But the wall between the two institutions has never been absolutistic in America.

In summary, the state relates to the symptoms of human sin in three ways: (1) it seeks to restrain them; (2) it embodies them because the power of the state is so immense and far-reaching that power is a continuing temptation to those who wield it; and (3) it is limited, even in its most creative efforts, by the corporate sin of humanity.[33] In the first instance the state exists to resist aggression against its citizenry from without and from within. In the second instance the American Constitution established an intricate set of legal checks and balances to safeguard against the state achieving absolute power. In the third instance the American government—like every other government—stumbles in its program of civil rights legislation, war on poverty, and foreign policy because of the corporate sin of humanity. Like all governments it is a temporal, finite, imperfect agency lacking omniscience, compassion, and redemptive power. Government is essential, but it must be adapted responsibly to serve human needs. The right of dissent (constitutionally guaranteed) is a built-in corrective in the democratic state.

The Continuing Interaction Between Church and State

The church, we have observed, influences the state indirectly and directly. We shall give consideration to several controversial direct influences in chapter 6 after identifying several indirect and direct influences in the remainder of this chapter.

Most significant of the indirect influences by the church is its long-range persuasive impact on the moral sensibilities and the value systems of the community. "Respect for persons, the value given to the family, the moral disciplines of the individual, a sense of social responsibility, the prodding of society to be open to truth and goodness, concern for the weak and disinherited, concern for offenders against society and the reconciling of enemies are effects of the long-term influence of the Christian Faith." [34] In this sense the church has had a long-term effect on the development of democracy in America. William Temple observed how dissenting English churchmen in the seventeenth century made a decided contribution to democratic government in England. In eighteenth-century England the Wesleyan Revival had a profound impact on the mores of English society. Specifically, the early Methodists called for the end of the slave trade, sent petitions to Parliament, and organized economic boycotts of products produced by slave labor.[35]

Another indirect influence of the church on the state occurs when the church is true to itself without seeking any clearly defined political purpose for the state. The church's insistence that it should be free to witness to the gospel has encouraged others to protect and enlarge their freedoms.[36] A primary example of this kind of influence is delineated by Roy F. Nichols. In his *Religion and American Democracy* he observes that "religion was destined to do more than mold the institutional forms of American Democracy. It was so to infuse the polity with its spirit that in time democracy itself was to resemble a religion." [37] The colonies were formed in many instances as acts of religious dissent. As the Great Awakening (1740-1760) swept the Atlantic seaboard, a fresh consideration of individualism emerged which, linked with the impact of rationalism from Europe, brought to the colonies the influence of deism and Locke and Newton. This political thinking fashioned the climate for revolution.

After the American Revolution there were continuous waves of religious experience (revivalism) until the late 1850s.[38] Through these recurring religious revivals the "preachers brought a new outlook on life, a new interpretation of the meaning of existence. Under orthodox Calvinism the individual was helpless; he was predestined either to be saved or damned. God had ordered his state from the beginning of time and he must obediently occupy the station to which it had pleased God to call him, for it was all for God's greater glory. But the appeal of the revivalist often was not in the static, helpless terms of Calvinism but in the exalting terms of the contrasting Arminian doctrine." [39] Nichols calls this crashing democracy of salvation "a tremendous revolution." [40] He is convinced that American historians have neglected "to give due consideration to the nature and consequences of this widespread and really tremendous experience which influenced and altered the lives of such a multitude. This period of recurring, almost constant, religious revival produced, in effect, what can be likened to another revolution, an Arminian Revolution. This emotional transformation had a terrific impact upon American society and upon the young democracy. It produced an equality such as no Declaration or Constitution, no statute, no law or decree could ever prescribe." [41]

The Arminian revolution made liberty available to all and established in the eyes of the American people the true equality of human life. This temper of mind spawned the temperance movement, encouraged the impulse for public education, and awakened and sustained the moral imperative to rid the nation of slavery. The Civil War itself was an assault of one subculture upon another, but "the dispute was formulated in moral-religious terms well understood in each." [42] The Northern religionists attacked the Southern religionists on the evil of slavery while the Southern moralists in turn attacked the Northerners for worshiping mammon and fostering a wage slavery more evil, they felt, than Negro slavery. The South also charged the North with breaking its word—the *covenant* of 1787—in attacking the sacred rights of the states. Each side judged its cause to be righteous. Both presidents addressed their legislative bodies in terms of firm belief in the righteousness of their particular cause. Davis, speaking first, explained the Confederacy's struggle in terms of the protection of the sacred rights of social contract against a willful and unscrupulous aggression.[43] Lincoln defined the contest as one to preserve the right of self-government. "The government of the United States," by his definition, "was the people's government with the responsibility of elevating the condition of men, to afford all a fair chance. The war was being fought to protect this unique experiment against a disgruntled minority who were striving to destroy it." [44] Mr. Lincoln concluded his defense of the war in this fashion: "And having thus chosen our course, without guile, and with pure purpose, let us renew our trust in God, and go forward without fear, and with manly hearts." [45] Both sides went to war in the name of liberty and righteousness; both claimed God's blessing. The church, having contributed to the climate of escalating righteous conflict, divided, and each became an active ally of the subculture in which it existed.

A third kind of indirect influence exercised by the church on the state is accomplished through "the teaching of its members about the meaning of Christian faith for great public issues of the day." [46] In earlier chapters, especially chapter 4, we cited extensive examples of this type of indirect influence on public education, slavery, abuse of labor, political reform, war and peace, civil rights, poverty, etc.

The distinction between indirect influence and direct action by the church cannot be absolutized. A shifting constitutional boundary rather than a high brick wall separates church and state in America. Direct forms of action often merge with indirect forms. Types of direct action are definable. We shall identify several here and examine them more closely in chapter 6.

(1) The several churches can assemble cooperatively for joint witness through local, state, national, and world councils. (2) Commissions authorized by any one of these several councils can be created and financed by the member churches to study and speak on specific issues. (3) Social and political issues can be spoken to directly by denominational bodies (national church conventions, houses of delegates, synods, congregations). (4) Denominational commissions or committees can speak for themselves. (5) Church leaders (bishops, synod presidents, pastors) can speak to or for their constituencies by virtue of their office. (6) Church leaders can speak for themselves but in the context of their office. (7) Denominational and Catholic bodies and church councils can lobby in state and federal governments. (8) At all levels of the institutional church direct services and support can be provided to minorities, disoriented youth, the poor, etc.

A century ago Carl Schurz declared, "Our country right or wrong. When right, to be kept right; when wrong, to be put right." But what is "right" and "wrong" the church must determine in the light of God's Word, if it is to be true to its nature and purpose. Consequently, Christians are most contributory to the commonweal when they *are* the people of God—proclaiming the gospel, guarding apostolic truth, doing the truth, and rendering priestly service in the world. The Christian citizen speaks to the issues of his time and becomes involved in the action of his day, because he is constrained to by Christ who is concerned for the well-being of persons in the world.

Motivation for this thrust depends, in part, on political integrity in the church. This crucial issue, linked with an examination of the church's direct impact on political society, is the theme of the next chapter.

Chapter 6

POLITICAL INTEGRITY IN THE AMERICAN CHURCH

I am approached with the most opposite opinions and advice, and that by religious men who are equally certain that they represent the divine will. I am sure that either the one or the other class is mistaken in that belief, and perhaps in some respects both. I hope it will not be irreverent for me to say that if it is probable that God would reveal his will to others on a point so connected with my duty, it might be supposed he would reveal it directly to me; for, unless I am more deceived in myself than I often am, it is my earnest desire to know the will of Providence in this matter. And if I can learn what it is, I will do it.

—Abraham Lincoln

From colonial days to the present, politics and piety have been intertwined, Christ and culture have interacted, church and state have influenced each other institutionally in American history. Civic piety and religion-in-general have evolved alongside the confessional and sectarian religions. Wherever politics is, piety is never far behind, and vice versa in American history. Religious fervor contributed heavily to the shaping of political concepts and social movements in America: the American Revolution, manifest destiny, the Civil War, the Progressive Era, the civil rights movement, etc. Dissent and violence have been—and are—firm strands in America's national character and history, and churchmen have helped to fashion both.

For three hundred years America was a "righteous empire," first in the making and then "on the make." Violence was employed to maintain the status quo more often than it was used to redress local, national, and international injustices against humanity. In most instances the church accepted, concurred in, and/or actively supported the nation-state (or a particular section of the nation-state) in those repressive acts. American politicians have persuaded and manipulated church members to support class, racial, and other disruptive national purposes. Broadly, too, the state itself has used the church. Through its public education system the state "is and always has been teaching religion. It does so because the well-being of the nation and the state demands this foundation of shared beliefs. . . . In this sense the public school system of the United States *is* its established church." [1] Robert Michaelson, commenting on the "fourth R" (religion) in education declares: "The pupil in the public school has been taught to read . . . in order . . . that he might be a pious person, or a moral man, or a loyal citizen." [2]

The church has also used the state to accomplish some of its purposes. Politicians have been loath to challenge church member-citizens on issues that would jar their piety. Only recently did the Supreme Court challenge the "Protestant ethic" in disallowing Bible reading and prayer in the public schools. The furor among the citizenry was intense. Politicians have been equally loath until recently to offend Catholic piety where it touches on parochial education, birth control, abortion laws, etc. Both the Protestant and the Catholic Churches have used the state to foster and/or safeguard their teachings. The Constitution explicitly states only this: The government shall *not establish any religion or impose any religious test for the holding of public office.* Churchmen in America are simply exercising their constitutional rights when they dissent from governmental policies or advocate specific policies for governmental enactment. On the other hand, politicians are not required to favor any particular religion.

The American nation-state, when it considers its sovereignty threatened, resists and, on occasion, coerces persons of conscience and independent judgment. Churchmen committed to the gospel of God cannot escape collision with the democratic sovereign state on some issues. So long as the state provides order with widening justice for all people, it deserves critical support; that is Paul's argument in Romans. John agrees (Revelation), adding specifically that when the state usurps God's place, its claims must be resisted. That is an elemental Christian response whether it be in the Roman state in the second century, the Nazi state in the 1930s and 40s, or in a United States exercising hegemony in Vietnam. Jesus' dictum, "Render unto Caesar . . ." puts these complementary views into a single argument calling for critical loyalty to both church and state with ultimate loyalty to God.[8]

The church acts on the state indirectly and directly. In this chapter we are concerned with its direct action on the state through denominational and interdenominational studies, statements, and lobbying. James L. Adams, investigating "the growing church lobby in Washington," for example, reports with obvious alarm that "the major Protestant denominations . . . and the Roman Catholic Church spend more than a million dollars annually to operate their Washington offices and pay their professional staffs. . . . The church lobby is as firmly entrenched now on the capital landscape as the Washington Monument. Yet the man in the pew is abysmally unaware of what his denomination is doing there." [4]

Some church ultra-liberals have been arrogant in their demands for change in the institutions of both church and state. They assume little responsibility for persuading and equipping other churchmen to be effective in the process of social change; disregarding their contrary views, they simply confront them. Nathan Pusey accused a handful of student radicals of employing McCarthy tactics in accomplishing their ends at Harvard in 1970. A similar charge might be launched against a handful of church liberals who insist that any view other than their own is "unchristian." Violence against the human spirit is not less damaging than violence against the human body. Some ultra-liberals, impatient to achieve their goals, write off the parish, the denomination, and institutional Christianity itself.[5] Their high-handedness, arrogance, and ill-concealed disdain of churchmen who adopt another style of witness have antagonized millions of churchmen, some of whom should and could have been persuaded to social involvement.

At the other end of the spectrum are religious conservatives who argue that the church must stay out of politics altogether. Will Campbell and Arthur Holloway, disillusioned by the results of their political activism, opt for this view.[6] Jacques Ellul is also convinced that the church cannot effect change through political channels. Nonetheless, the National Association of Evangelicals (NAE)—conservatives whose churches "profess to subscribe to faith in the 'Bible as the inspired, the only infallible, authoritative word of God'" and to other fundamental Christian doctrines—engages in political lobbying on issues which concern them directly.[7] And on the far right, Carl McIntire and thousands of ultra-fundamentalist churchmen insist that "the ministry of the church is to be missionary, not governmental."[8] Yet McIntire's *Christian Beacon* is politically oriented in issue after issue. He is raucously outspoken and vigorously active for the political policies he approves.[9] His vigorous prosecution of the Vietnam war has earned him the title "Cannonball" McIntire.

In many socio-political situations some liberals, moderates, conservatives, and ultra-fundamentalists in the church can be charged with bad faith and inept politics as they seek a direct influence on the state.

At the Congregational Level

There is glaring incongruity in congregations (and groups of congregations and councils of churches) which call for open housing, equal employment, equal educational opportunities, the alleviation of poverty, and the making of peace, while they minister uncritically to comfortable (affluent) middle-class, white-collar, chauvinistic Caucasian members.[10] Since politics is the art of establishing and maintaining order and achieving a degree of justice for all citizens, congregations which espouse social justice without motivating their members to promote justice in their own community by specific congregational actions which enlarge justice in that community are guilty of bad faith and dishonest politics. The chasm between what ought to be, and can be, at the congregational level is bridgeable only if conversion and enlightenment occur on a broad scale in congregation after congregation.[11] A radical change at the grass roots is imperative.

That is not likely to happen unless congregation after congregation faces up to and forsakes its ingrained disposition to orient to illusion rather than reality. Next, it must distinguish between the *strategy* and the *tactics* of ongoing renewal and deepening involvement in the world. Biblically viewed, there is one central strategy: the community of faith (the church) is called *out* of the world to become equipped to serve *in* the world. Each person is free to accept Christ's lordship in his life and situation or to ignore, reject, or attack the Word and its bearer. Any tactic which implements and advances this strategy of service in *any* place at *any* time is acceptable to God and advantageous to man, privately and publicly. This basic strategy roots in biblical theology. Its implementation requires faith, hope, professional competence, and political integrity.

For example, both clergy and laity must learn to treat one another as persons called by God to serve persons rather than as objects to be manipulated, intimidated, or coerced. These unchristian practices are rampant in the grass-roots church as well as in the ecclesiastical bureaucracies. Some concrete questions must be answered specifically in each local congregation. Do the lay leaders regard their clergy as bold spokesmen for God or as managers paid to serve the narrow self-interests of a power bloc in the congregation? Does the official board view its staff as hired hands to be "had" at modest salaries? In congregations which believe that the laborer deserves his wages, the official board enlists an adequate staff, reviews their competence annually, remunerates them accordingly, and provides for their growth in professional competence. Where that is not possible (economically deprived areas, mission congregations, experimental ministries) denominations or cooperative church bodies should subsidize these local ministries responsibly or decline to initiate them. The church's political ineptitude in these areas negates its witness to a God who cares about persons.

Secular man ignores a church which provides sanctuary for incompetent professionals. He recoils from a church which expects competent lay and clerical workers to endure economic hardship in an affluent society. In many places the church adheres to a business ethic which is inferior to that practiced in the business community, yet carps moralistically at the competitive economic society. The truth is that many able clergy, like creative teachers, are shamefully underpaid. In an affluent society this means that they are undervalued. It is this dehumanization which causes many able clergy and teachers to lose heart and discourages highly gifted men and women from taking up either profession.

But if some laity view their clergy as objects to be manipulated, exploited, and tolerated, it is equally true that some clergy look on the laity as objects. Some pastors decry the limitations of their parishioners instead of accepting, instructing, and shepherding them in a vital relationship with Christ and leading them into cooperative ventures designed to build a more humane society. Such clergy are neither politic nor biblical. The lawyer does not complain that his client is in trouble with the law. He is politic. The accountant does not complain that his client's records are a mess. He accepts this as his work. The medical doctor does not complain that his patient is ill. He knows this is his responsibility. Yet many clergy complain that the laymen committed to their pastoral care are recalcitrant, ignorant, parochial, ungenerous, and uninvolved. That is slothful and irresponsible. Church administrators (bishops and synodical and conference presidents), instead of confronting and counseling these clergy, usually shuffle them into other parishes where most continue to respond neurotically to strong-minded (occasionally neurotic) laymen. That is bad politics as well as bad theology. The growing practice of counseling these clergy and providing them with opportunities to enlarge their professional competence and improve their emotional health is a clear evidence that intelligent politics as well as pastoral concern are not wholly absent in the institutional church.

On the other hand, there are clergy who get totally involved in legitimate efforts to change social structures. Some use these commendable activities to escape the arduous work of caring for church members and equipping and nurturing *them* for service in the world—which is the church's essential task. Some clergy find it less demanding to join protest movements than to prepare biblically grounded, socially relevant sermons which persuade church members that *all* the people of God must witness in the world. It is less demanding for some clergy to participate in peace rallies than to counsel face to face with church members who truly think that protest movements are inspired by revolutionaries, Communists, and "kooks." Actually, the church must engage in both tasks; either without the other is a fractured ministry. Certainly, it is politically unsound.

There are clergy who enlarge church facilities at the expense of the congregation's servant role in the community or labor shortsightedly to keep doors open in faltering congregations which are social enclaves or cultic societies. Parish pastors, seminary professors, and church executives must come to terms with a deep-rooted ecclesiastical schizophrenia which has separated preaching from pastoral ministry, teaching from pastoral counseling, social action from biblical witness, and the efficient administration of an institution from the pastoral care of persons. This current schizophrenia is bad theology and inept politics. Until the clergy see themselves as persons called and ordained to help other persons meet Christ in the Scriptures, in worship, the sacraments, preaching, and the world, and as persons called to equip laymen to render priestly service to their fellowmen and to fashion social institutions which are hospitable to humanity, the church, seeking to speak on public issues, will carry little weight among its own members and none in the world.

The purpose of being openly politic at the congregational level is not an end in itself. The purpose is not simply to have an organization in which the gears run smoothly, but to build a fellowship of the committed and concerned which serves persons effectively in the world. In such a fellowship persons value persons because the person of Christ is valued above all. Congregations in which political integrity is a reality can speak persuasively to and act honestly upon social (political) issues in the community, city, state, and nation.

There is also a pressing need to practice intelligent politics between and among congregations and denominations in the same community. The day of the isolated or competitive congregation or denomination is gone. The politics of merger, cooperative ministry, and regional witness—implied in the gospel—is dictated by the changing socio-economic situations which now prevail in urban, suburban, and many rural areas. Here, too, honest politics will enlarge the church's effective witness. Realistic secularists have much to teach the church about shared responsibility.

Honest politics is also indispensable in the strengthening of local councils of churches, the establishing of area parish councils, and the developing of regional (as contrasted with national bureaucratic) ministries. Where there is openness and candor, Protestant, Catholic, and Orthodox ministries will fashion cooperative ventures to serve God and man. At the same time these working units will cooperate eagerly with Jewish and secular agencies in concrete ventures designed to produce a more humane society. The dangers in this unprecedented flexibility are obvious, but the potential gains require these risks in faith. Wherever people find common answers to pressing social problems, they will also find a deeper sense of community.[12] That is constructure politics. If, however, cooperative ventures are undertaken simply to prolong the life of ineffective local ministries or because the clergy consider it an "in" thing, those acts do not reflect political integrity.[13]

At the Denominational Level

Keith Bridston, professor of theology at the Pacific Lutheran Seminary and a pioneer writer on church politics, declares: "If I were to pinpoint the difference between church and secular politics, I would say that the former is less honest. . . . To call church politics 'dishonest' is only another way of saying that church politics has tended to be hidden and camouflaged and thus denied. Modern psychoanalytic insight has helped us to see that such repression is not only a symptom of sickness but also a cause. . . . In church politics we must confess, with Freud, that 'we are all sick.' " [14]

Church politics is hidden, camouflaged, and denied at the synodical (diocesan, district, presbyterial) and national denominational levels. Most churches at the regional and national levels employ "the ecclesiastical ballot," a device inherited from the Roman Church. There are no political parties, no avowed candidates, no nominating speeches, no political platforms, no debates, no discussions, and supposedly no electioneering. The first ballot is a nominating ballot. The persons named thereon become the candidates on the second ballot. In some ecclesiastical bodies the front-runners (perhaps four) compete on the third ballot; the fourth ballot pits the two front-runners against each other. A fifth ballot calls for a simple majority. In other churches the balloting—and the caucusing and electioneering—go on interminably until weariness or deals produce a winner. The assumption in all situations is that the Holy Spirit directs the voters to the ablest leader. In reality the predecessor's "choice" or a "name" churchman in the denomination is elected; or a popularity contest ensues; or a wheeling-dealing choice is made. Usually, the result is attributed piously to the Holy Spirit. In any event the electee and his supporters have been campaigning for months, sometimes years, while pretending otherwise. The harsh, behind-the-scenes election of the present executive secretary of the World Council of Churches is a case in point. Another example was the election of the president of the Lutheran Church—Missouri Synod in 1969. The wounds inflicted by both elections have not yet healed. The Christian Church is maimed severely by politics that are camouflaged, hidden, and deceptive. Bridston argues cogently that the absence of open politics in the church "is the strongest political guarantee for the perpetuation of the *ancien régime* and the most solid base for the continuation of the political establishment." [15]

Further, since voting is only the final stage in any election process, it is either done ignorantly or on hearsay evidence in church conventions. The candidates have not declared themselves publicly; the convention has heard no proposals from the candidates; open discussion of issues has not occurred. The delegates, enjoying a holiday in a convention city, buy a pig in a poke, vote for a "name," and/or, taking the path of least resistance, vote for the incumbent or his groomed man. In earlier days the ecclesiastical ballot had viability in small, intimate church units. But present-day ecclesiastical bodies are, in their fashion, as bureaucratic as government and education. Power gravitates into the hands of a bureaucratic elite who are rarely in touch with the grass-roots church, the electorate; the bureaucrats are insulated against political pressures.[16] This widespread situation has produced, and continues to produce, many of the anti-institutional neuroses which now prevail among the laity, especially the young. Bridston makes the pertinent observation that "the increase in the size and complexity of modern institutions, including the churches, makes inevitable greater bureaucratic development. As in so many other sectors of modern society, the 'experts' are in control. The managerial elite of the ecclesiastical machines are almost completely beyond popular political control." [17]

Bridston is on target. The church is mundane as well as sacred; politics and piety need to be joined openly in the church. To a substantial degree the alienation of clergy and laity from the institutional church stems from inept and/or dishonest politics among church bureaucrats. The current crunch in the churches, like its counterpart in society, roots in a complex of causes, but one cause certainly is the lack of openness, the absence of free discussion, and the hidden political maneuvering in the church itself.[18]

"The church is both a spiritual fellowship (*koinonia*) and a political institution (*ekklesia*)." [19] It will speak with larger honor—and certainly with deeper persuasiveness—to the institutions of society (family, education, government) if it sets its own house in order. A bureaucratic church cannot speak prophetically to a bureaucratic government. It is, in fact, dishonest for paid church "managers" to demand leadership rather than management in Congress and from the office of the President when they practice what they admonish others to disavow. Instinctively, young people and perceptive adults are critical and distrustful of the church as well as the state in this era. A new level of political integrity is required in both institutions to enable them to function honorably and to restore public confidence.

National and International Church Councils

"Who speaks for the church?" asks Paul Ramsey in his critique of the 1966 Geneva Conference on Church and Society, convened under the auspices of the World Council of Churches.[20] Ramsey, a social ethicist, cannot be pigeonholed as a liberal or conservative churchman. Some who argue that politics and piety can be compartmentalized claim Ramsey for support. That is not fair to the man or his arguments.[21] To avoid any possible misunderstanding, Ramsey states plainly that "we ought not to yield to those who say the church should stay out of politics. That's as undifferentiated as the way too often we now get into politics."[22] He is critical of *how* the church gets into politics; he insists that the biblical tradition should motivate and guide the church in this activity.

What Ramsey expects from national and international church bodies is *direction* for decisions in the political arena rather than *directives* for specific political action. He judges that the latter is "a form of culture-Christianity, . . . secular sectarianism."[23] In his judgment the practice negates a true prophetic witness to the transcendent God which constrains men to speak words of judgment "against both Baalism and the Baalization of Yahwehism."[24] The church should not recommend but clarify "the grounds upon which the statesman [political] must put forth his own particular decree."[25] Ramsey argues that the religious communities should be concerned with perspectives on politics.[26] He is convinced that "if the churches have any special wisdom to offer here, it is in cultivating the political ethos of a nation. . . . The church's business is not policy formation. That is the awesome responsibility of magistrates (and churchmen along with other citizens in their nonecclesiastical capacities)."[27] Ramsey believes that "the political conscience of the nation would be aided more, and particular decisions more instructed, if there were fewer judgments emanating from the churches upon specific cases, delivered as if these were the only conclusions to be reached from considerations of morality." [28]

Much that Ramsey says needs to be said. His central thrust is sound: the warrant for political action must be biblical. Most churchmen agree on that. These specific points which he makes also deserve critical consideration. Several are particularly relevant. (1) Some ultra-liberal churchmen, impatient with the grass-roots church's reluctance to live in the world, appear to have used the gospel to advance their social concerns. (2) Some have gone so far in particular statements on specific issues and events (Vietnam, the Chicago riots, busing, the election of 1964, etc.) as to imply that any churchman who does not agree with them is not Christian, an attitude which polarizes the church needlessly. (3) The church, overly eager to be relevant, has spoken too often on too many specific issues. (4) The church should concentrate on providing direction rather than specific directives if it wants to foster discussion in the congregations and in civil society. (5) The church must be mindful that the gospel is not relevant but irrelevant (immediately) to every culture and society.

But there is a thin line between giving *direction* and providing *directives*. What one man calls direction another calls a directive. Ramsey himself declines to get bogged down in this sticky but inescapable issue. Many churchmen, sobered and challenged by the Princeton professor's critiques, are not fully persuaded by his arguments on this issue. They judge that the church has not said too much but too little, and often too late, on specific social ills. They know from history and experience that the church will speak ill-advisedly, incompetently, and ignorantly on occasion. Luther, Calvin, Wesley, and the Roman popes erred on some socio-political issues, but they spoke. Many contemporary churchmen consider that the larger sin is not to speak, to speak belatedly, or to speak unspecifically. The 1966 Geneva Conference wrestled with man in society. Some of its documents are vacuous; others are grimly relevant, intensely pertinent, jarringly realistic. The church must speak. So long as every churchman and citizen has the freedom to modify, reject, or endorse ecclesiastical pronouncements in the light of his understanding of the gospel, church bodies should issue responsible statements to precipitate public discussion.[29] The time for the church to speak is not at the gate of Auschwitz but before the camp is erected.[30]

Helmut Thielicke, like Paul Ramsey, is also cautious about general church pronouncements on political issues. He argues that the church must, from the gospel, motivate persons who will then perceive and act on their responsibility to reorder society. But that view has proved to be less than adequate in the modern nation-states.[31] Suppose the American church had taken up the cause of labor in 1886. Suppose the German church had spoken corporately and specifically to the Nazi state in 1934 and shared its judgments with the world community of Christians. Suppose the Vatican had spoken for the Jews in Hitler's state in 1937. Suppose the American church had spoken concertedly against the Vietnam war in 1963. Suppose the American church had given more than sporadic support to welfare reform which the Congress buried in 1970. In each case it is conceivable that a significant historical impact would have been made. At the very least, the image of a church that cares about persons would have been projected in the world; the church's prophetic utility would have been exercised. Consquently, it is our judgment that the church has not said too much in the twentieth century, but that it has said too little—and attempted to accomplish too little. Substantially, the contemporary church is allied with a political society that opts for the status quo and actively suppresses dissent.

Further, the notion that congressmen, cabinet members, and presidents are supermen is absurd. It is obviously true that they possess inside factual information. But the notion that their instincts and judgments are superior to the instincts and judgments of all other citizens, including churchmen, is false. Elected representatives need to hear what all segments of society, including the church, think and feel on all basic issues. They need directives as well as direction from the citizenry. If they cannot cope with this kind of "pressure," they are not qualified to hold public office in a democracy. Lincoln, in spite of his lament (cited at the beginning of this chapter) would not have issued the Emancipation Proclamation in 1862 without a pressing popular *directive*. The Civil Rights Act of 1964 required the citizens' *direct* endorsement to be enacted. It is unlikely that Lyndon Johnson would have stepped down in 1968 if a substantial bloc of citizens had not directed him to do so. Vigorous dissent and plain directives, as well as counsel and direction, are essential to the effective working of any democratic government.

Built-in provisions for vigorous criticism are among the more significant characteristics for renewal in our democratic political system. But why should the majority be so considerate of political criticism and dissent? "To answer that question is to state one of the strongest tenets of our political philosophy. We do not expect organizations or societies to be above criticism, nor do we trust the men who run them to be adequately self-critical. We believe that those aspects of a society that are healthy today may deteriorate tomorrow. We believe that power wielded justly today may be wielded corruptly tomorrow." [32] That was the temper of mind that framed our Constitution; that was the spirit that fostered the first Ten Amendments, the American Bill of Rights.

Finally, the demands of God underlie the historical necessity for directives on specific issues. In every historical situation prophetic opposition to any government's inhuman policies is inherent in the church's commitment to the gospel. Joshua opposed his people's demand for a nationalistic war; he declared flatly that it was contrary to God's purpose. Jeremiah was rejected by his community because he spoke for God in concrete social and political terms. Amos and Micah were jarringly specific about God's demand for justice to the poor. John the Baptist lost his head, literally, because he issued a directive concerning Herod's immoral behavior. Jesus, accepting the woman taken in adultery as a person, forgave her; he also directed her to sin no more. He called King Herod "that fox," the Pharisees "whited sepulchers," and forcibly ejected the moneychangers from his Father's house. Directives as well as direction have a firm place in Christian faith and life. Both law and gospel comprise God's Word.

Who speaks for the church? Any person who counts himself among the people of God is *constrained* by God to speak and humbly to submit his pronouncements to the tribunal of biblical evidence. There have been and are single voices: John,

Peter, Augustine, Luther, John XXIII, Stringfellow, Berrigan, Groppe. There have been and are sectarian voices: the Lollards, the Quakers, the Brethren. There have been and are denominational and council voices speaking for selective conscientious objection, civil rights, welfare reform, the humanization of life. These voices can claim the authority of biblical tradition. There have been and are persons, churches, councils, commissions, and conferences constrained by Scripture's witness to express their moral and ethical concern over revolutionary movements in South Africa, Vietnam, China, and Brazil. Each church member and each citizen must judge whether the voice speaking is God's or man's. But unless the church speaks, there is no way of knowing either. The church is under biblical constraint, living in the world, to speak to the world in concrete terms. It is the church's responsibility to speak and act through persons, sects, denominations, and councils of churches. It will speak irresponsibly on occasion; that is inevitable because it is a divine-*human* instrument. Its lobbying for Prohibition is a case in point. But it can only prove the rightness of its judgment or discern the wrongness of it in the crucible of historical experience. When the church is true to the gospel, it dares boldly to risk.

Because social questions become political issues and because churchmen are citizens, the vital church will express its views publicly, bring them to the attention of government officials and, like other segments of American society, lobby for them. That is proper constitutional exercise. It is also an authentic biblical activity. Church lobbying is one firm means among many, and it is not new. The Methodists have maintained a building and staff at 100 Maryland Avenue, N.W., Washington, D.C., for fifty years for that purpose. James L. Adams has studied the growing church lobby in Washington.[33] His report should be examined by clergy and laity alike for reliable information *and* as a foil for a reasoned response. Charles Taft, skilled politician and respected liberal churchman, wrote the introduction to Adams' book; they are fellow Cincinnatians.[34] Mr. Taft states unequivocally that there is much in Adams' book with which he disagrees. He does suggest, as we have too in this chapter, that the current crunch in the churches might be less severe if more clergy were to get in touch with the laity and persuade them to get where the action is before galloping off alone to every fire on the social action front. Adams believes that the church should be a restrained political lobbyist serving only its institutional interests. In the political arena it should be a moral persuader. He judges that the church's current "political" activity is dividing the pulpit from the pew.

There are serious weaknesses in Adams' study. He does not orient to a biblical doctrine of the church. He is naïve about the decision-making processes of government. He assumes that all elected and appointed public officials know more on every issue than informed churchmen who lobby. Our first two criticisms have been documented in chapters 3-5. A vigorous criticism of Adams' third point can be summarized from the arguments of Herman Will, Jr., head of the Division of World Peace, Board of Social Concerns of The United Methodist Church, Washington, D.C.

First, public officials are limited in their freedom to act by parameters established by public opinion or their understanding of public opinion. How can federal officials correctly gauge such opinion if churchmen, on principle, abstain from expressing their convictions to their congressmen? . . .

Second, policy decisions by government officials are never made in a vacuum. Individuals and groups, inside and outside government, who are interested in the outcome, always have and always will seek to affect decisions. . . . Should churchmen abstain from attempting to influence public policy and leave the field to others whose actions may reflect primarily their own self-interest rather than any concern for the public interest?

Third, general church staff members, church members, and leaders may possess the educational background, training, and experience that qualify them to make an informed and expert judgment on the policy at issue, at least as well as, and in some cases better than the particular government officials involved. . . .

Fourth, public officials, even if technically competent, may overlook humanitarian or ethical considerations which should properly enter into a policy decision. . . .

Seventh, government officials engaged in a particular area of work tend to become increasingly specialized. . . . *Many officials will say frankly that in most cases the intelligent and informed public has available the essential information on which government policy is based.*

Eighth, the experts, whether within or outside the government, often disagree in their analyses of situations, differ as to facts and vary in proposals for policy. In such instances, expressed public opinion, informed or uninformed, may be helpful, even decisive.[35]

Lobbying is a fixed feature in our democratic state. The

Federal Government is the most influential institution in our urban-technological society. Neither the care of persons nor the care of the earth is possible without regulatory and protective aid by the Federal Government. It is the only social institution that can cope with corporate giants like General Motors or manage significant environmental protection against the oil industry. Church people—commissioned and equipped to care for persons, the earth, and the quality of life—must lobby for their judgments and convictions like any other "special interest" group. The church, viewed biblically, exists to preach and teach Christ, guard apostolic truth, and make the world a place where man can become truly human. The latter task cannot be accomplished in an urban-technological society without enlightened, responsible government action. The church has a responsibility for seeing that that action occurs.

Of course, the conservative wing of Protestantism lobbies too.[36] Mr. Adams quotes Floyd Robertson, assistant to the general director of the National Association of Evangelicals. as saying, "Our involvement in government affairs pertains only to those things which directly affect the function of the church and its activities—missions, chaplains, taxes, education, and freedom of speech as it pertains to radio and jail ministries."[37] Presently the focus of the National Association of Evangelicals' lobbying is on matters which interest the church institutionally. But there is evidence that it will broaden.

It is imperative that a cooperative alliance be forged between main-line Protestantism and these earnest, conservative churchmen. The latter's massive Congress on Evangelism in Minneapolis in 1969 agreed that evangelism in the 1970s must be linked to social concerns. Significantly, Mr. Robertson has stated: "We will . . . encourage the introduction of legislation which we feel to be of particular interest to the church as a whole or to *individuals as citizens*." [38] The evangelicals' fortnightly journal, *Christianity Today,* hints at open doors for cooperative addressment with main-line Protestantism on social issues. It is essential that mutual respect and cooperation be fostered between earnest evangelicals and main-line Protestant churches during the 1970s. A rapprochement there, as well as cooperation with the Roman Catholics, is crucial to Protestantism's "coming of age" as a concerned, catholic community in a technological society. Equally, Jews and humanists must be respected allies, too. The Judeo-Christian tradition has been a validating force in the American experiment. Its authority must be recovered and reasserted.

We are not advocating a syncretistic religion; we are calling for cooperative, concerted action in the face of human need— an affirmation of the biblical tradition. Each community can reassess its own tradition, gain insight into its brothers' traditions, and get on with God's work here and now. It is in doing that work, as well as in dialoguing about traditions, that true community comes into being.

We have recognized that some church liberals on the far left are arrogant, divisive, and militant; and that other liberals, moderates, and conservatives are involved directly in some political action. What is the record of the fundamentalists on the far right? [39] Are they as nonpolitical as they demand other churchmen to be?

Ultra-fundamentalism came into being through "the merging of the ultra-fundamentalist theology, which first appeared in the 1930s, and the political ideology of the far right, which was created in the late 1950s. These two currents were blended into a single stream by the leaders of ultra-fundamentalism about the time Senator John F. Kennedy announced his candidacy for the presidency of the United States." [40] The foundations for ultra-fundamentalism were laid during the quarter century (1920-1945) when the modernist-fundamentalist controversy reached its public heights in the Scopes "monkey trial" at Dayton, Tennessee, spawned the Machen controversy which upset Presbyterianism and loosed Carl McIntire, and prodded conservative churchmen to split into the National Association of Evangelicals and the American Council of Churches. Meantime, the Federal Council of Churches (later the National Council, 1951) became increasingly involved with social issues.[41]

The period 1945-57 was one of renewal and expansion for the ultra-fundamentalists (McIntire, Hargis, Bundy, and Kaub) and the conservatives as well. "The appearance of the World Council was interpreted by both the American Council and the National Association of Evangelicals as the most serious threat ever faced by traditional Christianity. That Council, in their judgment, embraced inclusivism, liberalism, members from Communist nations, critics of capitalism (as well as of Communism), and militant apostates." [42] McIntire's International Council of Christian Churches, a handful of churchmen opposing the World Council, gained extensive publicity from newsmen who were in Amsterdam in 1948 to report on the World Council. The reporters knew nothing of the new group's separationist history, but they considered that McIntire and his colleagues were issuing "newsworthy" statements ("the WCC is a tool of Moscow," etc.). Millions of people heard McIntire's name and charges for the first time. He spoke to the "paranoid" mind emerging in the late 1940s.[43]

McIntire and his religious colleagues were in tune with this political mind that was taking shape. The cold war was on; America was "righteous"; the Soviets were "evil"; China was a disappointment; Alger Hiss typified the horde of infiltrators in the government; the world was a mess! The American people wanted simple solutions to complex socio-economic-political problems. After all, that was their history, experience, and nature. The late Professor Hofstadter's description of this mind is sobering.

The American frame of mind was created by a long history that encouraged our belief that we have an almost magical capacity to have our way in the world, that the national will can be made entirely effective, as against other peoples, at a relatively small price. We began our existence without worldwide territorial aspirations or responsibilities, but as a continental power with basically continental aspirations. From the beginning of our national life, our power to attain national goals on which we were determined was in effect irresistible—*within* our chosen, limited, continental theater of action. Our chief foes—Indians, Mexicans, the decaying Spanish Empire—were on the whole easily vanquished. It is true that in fighting the British in 1812 we became engaged with a vastly greater power, but at a time when the British were in mortal combat with Napoleon and their American effort was a sideshow. Even then, though we did rather badly—our invasions of Canada were repulsed, our capitol was burned, and our shipping was bottled up—a curious stroke of luck at New Orleans made it possible for us to imagine that the stalemate peace we concluded represented some kind of victory. The only time the American land was truly ravaged by the horrors of war was during our own Civil War when our wounds were self-inflicted.[44]

With the persistence of this chauvinistic, unrealistic temper of mind, Joseph McCarthy was inevitable. McCarthy happened, as Hitler had happened, because of a fault in the national mind. The ultra-fundamentalists capitalized immediately on that political naïveté and social discord to advance their own narrow interests. In fact, they provided, through the office of J. B. Matthews, some of the material which Senator McCarthy used to shotgun the main-line churches.

Until 1964 the ultra-fundamentalists were absolute separationists. They attacked every agency, individual, or activity in sight: the National Council of Churches, the World Council of Churches, the National Association of Evangelicals, Billy Graham, Youth for Christ, denominational and interdenominational seminaries, the Revised Standard Version of the Bible, the United Nations, medicare, urban renewal, civil rights, public education, fluoridation, the progressive income tax (Sixteenth Amendment), public welfare, Earl Warren, Eisenhower, the Kennedys, Johnson, Nixon, and Communism.[45] A sampling of their official statements reveals a narow self-interest. (1) The McGuffey Readers of the nineteenth century should be reinstated in the public schools. Some "far right" bookstores stock the book.[46] (2) Children should be sent to private schools or to Shelton and Highland Colleges (ACCC institutions).[47] On Friday, January 15, 1971, the New Jersey Board of Higher Education voted unanimously to shut down McIntire's Shelton College in Cape May, New Jersey. Shelton, the State Board said, exhibited "substantial academic deficiencies coupled with a lack of institutional integrity and administrative competence." [48] Carl McIntire called the decision a "liberal frameup." [49] (3) The *Christian Beacon,* a McIntire publication, should be read regularly. In the *Beacon,* January 11, 1962, page 3, this description of one of America's most respected conservative preachers, Dr. Oswald Hoffman of the Lutheran Church—Missouri Synod, appears:

> An article such as is here presented could never have been written by a man who was forthright in his handling of Biblical truth in opposing Communism. . . . The Lutheran Hour has gone "soft" and if the view which it is presenting here of a positive opposition is accepted by the Lutherans generally, they will have departed from the spirit and militancy that was characteristic of Martin Luther in dealing with error.[50]

Another *Beacon* evaluation: *"The Lutheran,* published in Philadelphia . . . appears to be doing what it can to destroy the Christian religion." [51]

The stance of the ultra-fundamentalists has been and is compatible with the "paranoid" style in politics. Basic insight into understanding this segment in the church can be gained from this exchange of letters between E. Stanley Jones, renowned world missionary, and Carl McIntire after the latter had branded Jones "a missionary for a communistic new social order." [52] On Good Friday, April 7, 1950, Jones wrote to

McIntire: "Today we both stand before the judgment of the Cross. I pray that all that is in me that is unlike that Man, who hung on the Cross to redeem us with His own blood, may be taken out of me."

On April 10, McIntire replied: "I do not believe, Dr. Jones, that I now stand before the judgment of the Cross. Christ endured once and for all the wrath of God in judgment for me. I am freed from it all by His precious death."

On April 24, Jones wrote: "The cross means to you redemption, but there is no further judgment there for you. . . . You say it exalts you but does not humble you—does not judge you. In other words you feel that there is nothing in you that is not in harmony with the spirit of the Man who hung there. . . . You end in self-righteousness. . . . Not being judged by the Cross you then proceed to set up a judgment seat of your own . . . that makes you hard, censorious, critical. The pay-off is in you. You become what you give out." [53]

The ultra-fundamentalists gained strength and wielded wide influence during the McCarthy witch-hunts, but they really came into prominence on the coattails of John Kennedy and his "New Frontiersmen." Their fulminations, vituperations, and threatenings against Kennedy evoked this response from the President in a speech at Los Angeles in November, 1961:

In the most critical periods of our Nation's history, there have always been those on the fringes of our society who have sought to escape their own responsibility by finding a simple solution, an appealing slogan, or a convenient scapegoat. . . . They look suspiciously at their neighbors and their leader. They call for a "man on horseback" because they do not trust the people. They find treason in our churches, in our highest court, in our treatment of water. They equate the Democratic Party with the welfare state, the welfare state with socialism, socialism with communism. . . . Let our patriotism be reflected in the creation of confidence in one another, rather than in crusades of suspicion. . . . Above all, let us remember, however serious the outlook, however harsh the task, the one great irreversible trend in the history of the world is on the side of liberty.[54]

Political and religious extremism spread rapidly during the early 1960s. A series of events frenzied large sections of the country: Roman Catholic John Kennedy's election, the Bay of Pigs debacle, the Cuban missile crisis, the rising militancy of the blacks, the proposed civil rights legislation (1963), the government's sacking of Major General Edwin Walker for employing rightist indoctrination methods with American troops in Germany—and the assassination of President Kennedy. The ultra-fundamentalists reached their zenith of power and surrendered their separatist identity when they joined forces with the poltitical right in the election of 1964.

In the immediate aftermath of the assassination of John Kennedy, newsmen—recalling that a newspaper advertisement in a Dallas daily on the morning of Kennedy's visit had accused him of being Communist and that Dallas had long been a hotbed of political rightists—implied that the far right was responsible for the President's death. The Lee Oswald–Jack Ruby tragedy negated that premature judgment. But the implied charge gave the ultra-fundamentalists fresh ammunition. They demanded an apology, called Oswald a tool of Moscow, branded the Warren Commission a whitewash, attacked the Civil Rights Act of 1964, called for total victory in Vietnam, and pledged their active support to Senator Goldwater whose rightist forces had wrested the Republican presidential nomination from the Eastern Establishment. Goldwater's acceptance speech and the *Zeitgeist* provided the stage for one of the most virulent presidential campaigns in American history. "I would remind you," the candidate declaimed, "that extremism in the defense of liberty is no vice!" Once again, American "politics had been transformed into religion." [55]

Although the ultra-fundamentalists have declined through inner dissension and division since 1965, and McIntire and Hargis have fallen from their peak positions of 1964-1965, the right-wing segment in American politics remains very much alive. George Wallace's showing in the 1968 presidential race and his reelection as governor of Alabama, the revolt of the construction workers, and the tactics of Agnew-Nixon in 1970 are evidences of its vitality. Political-religious divisiveness in the 1970s is a Damocles' sword over a troubled nation.

The late Richard Hofstadter wrote prophetically in 1966:

The Right-Wing Enthusiasts . . . had less than nothing to show in practical results, *but it is not practical results that they look for.* They have demonstrated that the right wing is a formidable force in our politics and have given us reason to think that it is a permanent force. Writing in 1954, at the peak of the McCarthy period, I suggested that the American right wing could best be understood not as a neofascist movement girding itself for the conquest of power but as a persistent and effective minority whose main threat

181

was in its power to create "a political impossible." This still seems to be the true potential of the pseudo-conservative right; it is a potential that can be realized without winning the White House, even without again winning the Republican nomination. That the right-wingers are actually increasing in numbers is doubtful; but their performance in 1964 shows how much leverage they can achieve, whatever their numbers, with dedication and organization.[56]

It is not likely that ultra-fundamentalism is dead either. The prospects for political calm and internal peace are not sanguine for either church or state. The church—liberal, moderate, conservative, and ultra-conservative—has a long, hard road ahead before it achieves political integrity in its own ranks and inspires integrity in the political society in which it exists, serves, works, and witnesses. Political integrity is pragmatic and commonsensical in the church and society; equally, it is biblical and theological.

* * * * *

Wherever politics is in America, piety is not far behind. The 1960s wiped out any lingering illusion that the wall between church and state is absolute. The time is at hand for the development of a *new* piety informed by biblical theology and a *new* politics informed by sane public opinion. That will not happen in church or state apart from responsible dissent, conflict, reconciliation, meaningful dialogue, and radical changes in the structures and the spirit of both institutions. America has come of age in an era of unprecedented change. As Lincoln argued a century ago, the quiet dogmas of yesterday are not adequate guides in addressing today's issues and tomorrow's uncertainties. Both church and state need a rebirth of realism and hope. America's religious and political traditions—recovered, recast, and acted on—point the way. The current divisiveness in American society provides the reason. The Christian God offers the ground for hope.

NOTES

Preface

1. Oscar Cullmann, *The State in the New Testament* (New York: Charles Scribner's Sons, 1956), p. 3.
2. *Ibid.*, pp. 6-7.
3. Hugh Trevor-Roper, *The Rise of Christian Europe* (London: Thames and Hudson, 1965), p. 7.
4. Quoted in Pierre-Henri Laurent, "Paul-Henri Spaak and the Diplomatic Origins of the Common Market, 1955-1956," *Political Science Quarterly*, LXXXV (1970), 373-74.
5. *The Rise of Christian Europe*, pp. 9-10.

1: The Breaking Storm: Politics and Piety in Conflict

1. For example: William Lee Miller, "Piety Along the Potomac," *The Reporter*, August 17, 1954; A. Roy Burkhart, *The Surge of Piety in America* (New York: Association Press, 1954); Alan F. Geyer, *Piety and Politics* (Richmond: John Knox Press, 1963); "Piety and Politics," *Lutheran Forum*, III (November, 1970).

2. See Wallace E. Fisher, *From Tradition to Mission* (Nashville: Abingdon Press, 1965), chapter 3; *Preface to Parish Renewal* (Abingdon Press, Press, 1968) chapter 5; and *The Affable Enemy* (Abingdon Press, 1970).
3. New York: Harper & Row, 1969.
4. See Harold A. Bosley, "The Quiet Storm in the Churches," *The Christian Century*, December 2, 1970, pp. 1449-52. See also Lester Kinsolving, "Religion in the News," *The York Dispatch*, June 12, 1971.
5. See Erling Jorstad, *The Politics of Doomsday: Fundamentalists of the Far Right* (Nashville: Abingdon Press, 1970). See also Kenneth M. Dolbeare and Phillip E. Hammond, *The School Prayer Decisions: From Court Policy to Local Practice* (The University of Chicago Press, 1971).
6. *The School Prayer Decisions*, pp. 152-53.
7. See *Christianity and Crisis*, October, 1970.
8. Adams, *The Growing Church Lobby in Washington* (Grand Rapids: William B. Eerdmans Publishing Co., 1970), p. 13. We shall speak to this critique in chapter 6.
9. William Stringfellow and Daniel Berrigan are dramatic examples of this stance.
10. Paul Ramsey, *Who Speaks for the Church?* (Nashville: Abingdon Press, 1967); Helmut Thielicke, *Theological Ethics:* Vol. II, *Politics*, ed. William H. Lazareth (Philadelphia: Fortress Press, 1969); Will D. Campbell and James Y. Holloway, *Up to Our Steeples in Politics* (Paulist/Newman Paperback, 1970).
11. Thielicke, *Theological Ethics*, II, 648.
12. See Ramsey, *Who Speaks for the Church?*
13. See Langdon Gilkey, *How the Church Can Minister to the World Without Losing Itself* (New York: Harper & Row, 1964).
14. See *The Secular City Debate*, Daniel J. Callahan, ed. (New York: The Macmillan Co., 1966), and *Storm over Ethics* (New York: Doubleday & Co., 1967).
15. Bruce Larsen and Ralph Osborne, *The Emerging Church* (Waco, Texas: Word Books, 1970).
16. See Andrew Greeley, *The Crucible of Change: The Social Dynamics of Pastoral Practice* (New York: Sheed and Ward, 1968).
17. Adams, *The Growing Church Lobby in Washington*.
18. Laymen like William Thompson, William Stringfellow, Elton Trueblood, and Chad Walsh are exceptions who prove the rule.
19. Thomas Molnar, "The Shape of the Future: Are There New Political Concepts in the World Today? *Commonweal*, July 24, 1970, p. 365.
20. See Nils A. Dahl, "New Testament Eschatology and Christian Social Action," *The Lutheran Quarterly*, XXII (November, 1970).
21. See chapter 5 for a discussion on this religious-political tragedy.
22. See, for example, Sydney Mead, *The Lively Experiment* (New York:

Harper & Row, 1968), and Martin Marty, *Righteous Empire* (Harper & Row, 1970).

23. A judgment made by Professor Jerald Brauer, University of Chicago.

24. Abraham Lincoln, Annual Message to Congress, December 1, 1862.

25. John C. Bennett, *Christians and the State* (New York: Charles Scribner's Sons, 1958), p. 15.

26. See Wallace E. Fisher, *Can Man Hope to Be Human?* (Nashville: Abingdon Press, 1971), chapter 7, "Can the Church Help Man to Be Human?"

27. Mead, *The Lively Experiment,* chapters 1-4.

28. See Fisher, *Can Man Hope to Be Human?* Chapters 5-6.

29. Samuel Lubell, *The Hidden Crisis in American Politics* (New York: W. W. Norton & Co., 1970), p. 300.

30. Abe Fortas, *Concerning Dissent and Civil Disobedience* (New York: World Publishing Company, 1968). See also the Constitution, Article VI, and the First Amendment.

31. James Bouton, *Ball Four: My Life and Hard Times Throwing the Knuckleball in the Big Leagues* (Cleveland: World Publishing Co., 1970), p. 82.

32. James Michener, *The Quality of Life* (Philadelphia: J. B. Lippincott Co., 1970), p. 42.

2. The American Democratic State

1. Helmut Thielicke, *Theological Ethics,* II, 63-64.

2. See Carlton J. H. Hayes, *A Political and Cultural History of Modern Europe,* Vol. II (New York: The Macmillan Co., 1939).

3. The "Free French" and the "Free Poles" in England had national sentiment, community, etc., but they lacked political sovereignty. Viewed in that context, one can say that Charles DeGaulle became France.

4. That is the argument advanced by many youth, blacks, and poor whites. It is implicit in Charles Reich's *The Greening of America* (New York: Random House, 1970).

5. See W. F. Albright, *From Stone Age to Christianity* (New York: Harper & Row, 1948).

6. See George H. Sabine, *A History of Political Theory* (New York: Henry Holt and Co., 1948), pp. 3-19.

7. *Ibid.,* p. 63. See also Marshall Clagett, "The Medieval Heritage: Political and Economic," *Chapters in Western Civilization,* I (New York: Columbia University Press, 1948), 6-8.

8. Sabine, *A History of Political Theory,* p. 63.

9. *Ibid.,* p. 105.

10. William H. McNeill, *The Rise of the West* (Chicago: University of Chicago Press, 1963), pp. 444-46; and Clagett, "The Medieval Heritage: Political and Economic," pp. 12-17.
11. See M. P. Gooch, *Nationalism* (New York: The Macmillan Co., 1929).
12. See Preserved Smith, *The Age of the Reformation* (New York: The Macmillan Co., 1939); and Roland Bainton, *Here I Stand* (Nashville: Abingdon Press, 1950).
13. See Machiavelli's *The Prince*.
14. Hayes, *A Political and Cultural History of Modern Europe*, II.
15. Abraham Lincoln's Gettysburg Address is the most concise statement on political democracy in print. His Second Inaugural Address is the best single exposition of American civil religion.
16. This political theory was developed after the fact. John Locke, who influenced Jefferson's draft of the Declaration of Independence, framed his political theory after the "Glorious Revolution" of 1688 in England. Plato and Aristotle framed their political philosophies almost a century after "democratic" Athens destroyed itself in internecine strife with Sparta.
17. See chapter 4.
18. See Homer Carey Hockett, *Political and Social Growth of the American People, 1492-1865* (New York: The Macmillan Co., 1947), p. 156.
19. *Ibid.*, p. 157.
20. "Only in 1776 did *republic, republican and republicanism* change from defamatory clichés used to stigmatize critics of the existing order to terms with affirmative connotations, stimulating a feeling of identification with the existing political system. The reversal of the rhetorical value of these terms set in on January 9, 1776, with the publication of Thomas Paine's *Common Sense*." See W. Paul Adams, "Republicanism in Political Rhetoric Before 1776," *Political Science Quarterly*, LXXXV (1970), 397-421.
21. Patrick Henry, a firebrand instigator of revolution in the 1770s and the wartime governor of Virginia, refused to attend the Convention and thereafter labored diligently to prevent ratification of the Constitution in his state.
22. Hockett, *Political and Social Growth of the American People*, p. 287.
23. Roy F. Nichols, *The Disruption of American Democracy* (New York: The Free Press 1948), p. 7. The italics are mine.
24. Rhode Island declined to ratify the Constitution. It was forced into the Union when the other twelve states ratified the conservative document.
25. See Charles A. Beard, *An Economic Interpretation of the Constitution* (New York: The Macmillan Co., 1913).
26. See Wilfred Binkley, *American Political Parties, Their Natural History* (4th ed.; New York: Alfred A. Knopf, 1962).

NOTES

27. See Merrill D. Peterson, *Thomas Jefferson and the New Nation* (New York: Oxford University Press, 1970).
28. The terms "democrat" and "democratic" were derogatory descriptions in those days. The Jacksonian "revolution" made the terms respectable.
29. The proceedings at Hartford were secret. It has never been established precisely what the New Englanders had in mind. It is generally agreed, however, that secession was their intention.
30. See Wilfred Binkley, *American Political Parties,* chapters 1-4.
31. See Arthur M. Schlesinger, Jr., *The Age of Jackson* (Boston: Little, Brown, and Co., 1946). But it was not universal suffrage. Not until 1920 did females get the vote and not until 1970 did eighteen-year-old male and female citizens win the right to vote. The Negro, enfranchised after the Civil War, has only now won the right to vote in all states.
32. John Quincy Adams had declined in 1824 and during the next four years to deal in political patronage.
33. The Whiskey Rebellion, the Kentucky Resolutions, the Hartford Convention, and South Carolina's threatened "rebellion" were precursors of the Civil War. The American has always been impatient with authority.
34. Hockett, *Political and Social Growth of the American People,* p. 546.
35. *Ibid.,* p. 638.
36. See Bernard DeVoto, *The Year of Decision: 1846* (Boston: Little, Brown, and Co., 1943).
37. Nichols, *The Disruption of American Democracy,* pp. 16-29.
38. *Ibid.,* and Bruce Catton, *The Coming Fury,* Vol. I (Garden City, N.Y.: Doubleday and Co., 1961).
39. *The Disruption of American Democracy,* p. 505.
40. Many of the Confederate officers had fought in the Mexican War. Also, the aristocratic social system of the South was hospitable to the martial spirit and the development of military leaders.
41. The North had 61 percent of the population, 66 percent of the railroad mileage, 67 percent of the farms, 75 percent of the wealth produced, and 81 percent of the factories. Chart in Hofstadter, *et al., The United States History of a Republic,* p. 360. For two contemporary appraisals of Mr. Lincoln's broad capacities of leadership see T. Harry Williams, *Lincoln and His Generals* (New York: Alfred A. Knopf, 1952) and Burton J. Hendrick, *Lincoln's War Cabinet* (Boston: Little, Brown and Co., 1946).
42. William Seward advised Lincoln to wait for a military success before issuing the Proclamation. The stalemate at Antietam, Maryland, in September, 1862, provided the occasion for the historic pronouncement.
43. See the *Report of the National Advisory Commission on Civil Disorders* (New York: Bantam Books, 1968).

44. Lincoln received 55 percent of the popular vote. Although the electoral vote was a landslide, 212-21, almost half the voters in the North wanted the President ousted. For a "rebel" view of the disintegration of the Southern cause, see John B. Jones, *A Rebel War Clerk's Diary,* ed. Earl Schenck Miers (New York: Sagamore Press, 1958).

45. Bruce Catton, *Never Call Retreat, The Centennial History of the Civil War,* Vol. III (Garden City N.Y.: Doubleday and Co., 1965), p. 469.

46. The Democrats also bid for the popular general's services. Senator Lodge's preoccupation with the election of General Eisenhower opened the door to young John Kennedy, who won Lodge's place in the Senate. See Eric F. Goldman, *The Crucial Decade—And After, 1945-1960* (New York: Vintage Books, 1960), chapter 12.

47. See Richard M. Nixon, *Six Crises* (New York: The Macmillan Co., 1960).

48. Quoted in Ronald Segal, *The Americans: A Conflict of Creed and Reality* (New York: Viking Press, 1969), p. 259.

49. Daniel Boorstin, *The Decline of Radicalism* (New York: The Macmillan Co., 1969), pp. 107-11.

50. *Ibid.,* p. 108.

51. *Ibid.,* pp. 109-10.

52. Moyers, *Listening to America* (New York: Harper & Row, 1971), p. 7.

53. Boorstin, *The Decline of Radicalism,* p. 111.

54. *Ibid.*

55. See Joe McGinniss, *The Selling of the President, 1968* (New York: Trident Press, 1969).

56. *The Christian Century,* December 2, 1970, p. 1439.

57. *Ibid.* See also Peter F. Drucker, *The Age of Discontinuity* (New York: Harper & Row, 1968), especially chapters 1, 5, 6, 8, 10, 11, and 16. But is there any evidence that the machine (computer) can ever do more than the human brain programs for it?

58. James Michener, *The Quality of Life,* pp. 30-31.

59. *The Decline of Radicalism,* pp. 121-34.

60. See Reich, *The Greening of America,* for unhistorical, anti-intellectual expectations on the salutary impact of "Consciousness III." See Roger Starr, The Counter-Culture and Its Apologists: 2," *Commentary,* December, 1970, pp. 46-54, for a critique of Reich on "Consciousness III."

61. Boorstin, *The Decline of Radicalism,* p. 127.

62. *Cox Report on the Columbia Riots* (Professor Cox is professor of law at Harvard University).

63. See Harold E. Fey, "America's Most Oppressed Minority," *The Christian Century,* January 20, 1971, pp. 65-68.

64. "Do Students Want Education?" *Commonweal,* March 13, 1970, p. 11.

65. Eldridge Cleaver, *Soul on Ice* (New York: Dell Publishing Co., 1968), p. 61.
66. Haughton, *The Gospel Where It Hits Us* (Notre Dame, Ind.: Ave Maria Press, 1968), pp. 163-64.
67. Nichols, *The Disruption of American Democracy,* an exhaustive study of politics, 1856-1861, is instructive today.

3. The American

1. Quoted in D. W. Brogan, *Politics in America* (New York: Anchor Books, 1960), pp. 413-14.
2. Michael Wallace, "The Uses of Violence in American History," *The American Scholar,* XL (1970-71), 102.
3. Richard Hofstadter and Michael Wallace, eds., *American Violence, A Documentary History* (New York: Alfred A. Knopf, 1970), p. 475.
4. D. W. Brogan points out that the Constitution of the Confederate States of America was an exact copy of the Constitution of the United States of America, except for the added phrase "under God" (*Politics in America,* p. 6). Obviously, the addition of the pious phrase did not guarantee the success of Confederate arms.
5. See Nichols, *The Disruption of American Democracy.*
6. Roy F. Nichols, *Religion and American Democracy* (Baton Rouge: Louisiana State University Press, 1959), pp. 84-95. We shall discuss this more fully in chapter 5.
7. Wallace, "The Uses of Violence in American History," pp. 81-82.
8. Hector de Crevecoeur, *Letters from an American Farm* (New York: Fox, Duffield & Co., 1904), p. 54. Quoted in Merle Curti, *The Growth of American Thought* (New York: Harper & Row, 1943), pp. 3, 11.
9. Mead, *The Lively Experiment.* Mead quotes George Santayana, *Character and Opinion in the United States* (New York: Charles Scribner's Sons, 1920), p. 168: "They have all been uprooted from their several soils and ancestries and plunged together in one vortex, whirling irresistibly in a space otherwise quite empty."
10. Alexis de Tocqueville, *Democracy in America* (New York: The Macmillan Co., 1838), p. 1.
11. George W. Pierson, *Tocqueville and Beaumont in America* (New York: Oxford University Press, 1938), pp. 69-70.
12. Tocqueville, *Democracy in America,* p. 61.
13. Commager, *The American Mind* (New Haven: Yale University Press, 1959), p. 163.
14. *Ibid.,* p. 165.
15. *Ibid.,* p. 164.

16. See Robert N. Bellah, "Civil Religion in America," *Daedalus,* Winter, 1967. Professor Bellah, a Harvard sociologist, argues that a civil religion exists in America and "has its own seriousness and integrity and requires the same care in understanding that any other religion does." Throughout this study we are concerned with civil religion (civil piety) as well as church-sect religion. For a critique of Bellah's argument, see John F. Wilson, "The Status of 'Civil Religion' " in Elwyn A. Smith, ed., *The Religion of the Republic* (Philadelphia: Fortress Press, 1971), pp. 1-21. He contends that there are obvious evidences of a "civic piety," but it has not yet been established that there is a "civil religion" *per se.* See also Will Herberg, *Protestant, Catholic, Jew: An Essay in American Religious Sociology* (Garden City, N.Y.: Doubleday and Co., 1960), and Conrad Cherry, *God's New Israel: Religious Interpretations of American Destiny* (Englewood Cliffs, N.J.: Prentice-Hall, 1971).

17. Brogan, *Politics in America,* p. 6. The italics are mine.

18. *The Greening of America,* p. 333. Professor Reich's analysis of our social situation is packed with insight. His solution, however, is romantic because like Rousseau he sees man (particularly the young) as intrinsically good, and society as essentially evil.

19. James Bryce, *The American Commonwealth,* I (London: Macmillan and Co., 1891), 1.

20. *Ibid.*

21. Brogan, *Politics in America,* p. 2.

22. Commager, *The American Mind,* p. 162.

23. Bryce, *The American Commonwealth,* I, 2.

24. *Ibid.,* p. 468.

25. See Wallace E. Fisher, "The Religious and Social Philosophy of Theodore Roosevelt" (unpublished Master of Arts dissertation, Department of History, University of Pittsburgh, 1945).

26. *Ibid.;* Micah 6:8, "What doth the Lord require of thee, but to do justly, and to love mercy, and to walk humbly with thy God?"

27. He sent the Navy around the world; presided at the peace negotiations between Japan and Russia, built the Panama Canal, engaged in trust-busting, etc.

28. Richard Hofstadter, William Miller, Daniel Aaron, *The United States, the History of a Republic* (Englewood Cliffs, N. J.: Prentice-Hall. 1957), pp. 567-68.

29. Christopher Lasch, *The New Radicalism in America, 1889-1963: The Intellectual as a Social Type* (New York: Alfred A. Knopf, 1965), pp. 13-14.

30. Arthur M. Schlesinger, Jr., *The Thousand Days* (New York: The Macmillan Co., 1966), p. 713.

31 Quoted in Frederick Paxson, *The Frontier in American History* (Cam-

bridge, Mass: Riverside Press, 1924). Paxson judged "that the frontier with its continuous influence is the most American thing in all America." Other historians have judged that American geographic security until the advent of nuclear weapons was equally influential on shaping the American experience. Both *natural* factors had an incalculable influence on the American mind.

32. The vast continent provided a socio-economic-political safety valve. Bounded by two oceans and weak neighbors, it also provided *national* security until the advent of nuclear weapons.

33. Hofstadter, *et al., The United States*, p. 457.

34. Commager, *The American Mind*, p. 41.

35. *Ibid.*

36. *Ibid.*, p. 406.

37. Herbert Marcuse, *Eros and Civilization* (Boston: Beacon Press, 1955), and *One Dimensional Man* (London: Routledge and Kegan Paul, 1964). Eldridge Cleaver, *Soul on Ice*. Charles Reich, in *The Greening of America*, announced the end of the second evolutionary stage (Consciousness I—rural America; Consciousness II—corporate America). See also James M. Gavin, *Crisis Now* (New York: Random House, 1965).

38. Series, "Are We in the Middle of the Second American Revolution?" *The New York Times Magazine*, May, 1970, p. 26.

39. *Ibid.*, p. 27.

40. *Ibid.*, p. 116.

41. Gibson Winter, *Being Free, Reflections on America's Cultural Revolution* (New York: The Macmillan Co., 1970), p. 6. See also Jacques Ellul, *The Technological Society* (New York: Alfred A. Knopf, 1964).

42. Snow, *Science and Government* (Cambridge: Harvard University Press, 1961). The italics are mine. To quote Snow more fully: "And when I say the 'cardinal choices,' I mean those which determine in the crudest sense whether we live or die. . . . For instance, the choice in England and the United States in 1940 and 1941, to go ahead with work on the fission bomb; the choice in 1945 to use that bomb when it was made."

43. Boorstin, *The Decline of Radicalism*, p. 3.

44. *Ibid.*, p. 4.

45. See Andrew Hacker, *The End of the American Era* (New York: Atheneum Press, 1970).

46. *The Pursuit of Loneliness* (New York: The Macmillan Co., 1970).

47. *Ibid.*, p. 4.

48. *No Easy Victories*, ed. Helen Rowan (New York: Harper & Row, 1968), p. 115.

49. T. S. Eliot had remarked on that loneliness a half century earlier in *The Cocktail Party*. David Riesman's *The Lonely Crowd* provided a

sociological examination of loneliness almost two decades ago. Contemporary movies underscore it poignantly—*Midnight Cowboy, Easy Rider, Joe*. Professor Slater's parable of the lonely American (1970) is devastating: "Once upon a time there was a man who sought escape from the prattle of his neighbors and went to live alone in a hut he had found in the forest. At first he was content, but a bitter winter led him to cut down the trees around his hut for firewood. The next summer he was hot and uncomfortable because his hut had no shade, and he complained bitterly of the harshness of the elements. He made a little garden and kept some chickens, but rabbits were attracted by the food in the garden and ate much of it. The man went into the forest and trapped a fox, which he tamed and taught to catch rabbits. But the fox ate up the man's chickens as well. The man shot the fox and cursed the perfidy of the creatures of the wild. The man always threw his refuse on the floor of his hut and soon it swarmed with vermin. He then built an ingenious system of hooks and pulleys so that everything in the hut could be suspended from the ceiling. But the strain was too much for the flimsy hut and it soon collapsed. The man grumbled about the inferior construction of the hut and built himself a new one. One day he boasted to a relative in his old village about the peaceful beauty and plentiful game surrounding his forest home. The relative was impressed and reported back to his neighbors, who began to use the area for picnics and hunting excursions. The man was upset by this and cursed the intrusiveness of mankind. He began posting signs, setting traps, and shooting at those who came near his dwelling. In revenge groups of boys would come at night from time to time to frighten him and steal things. The man took to sleeping every night in a chair by the window with a loaded shotgun across his knees. One night he turned in his sleep and shot off his foot. The villagers were chastened and saddened by this misfortune and thereafter stayed away from his part of the forest. The man became lonely and cursed the unfriendliness and indifference of his former neighbors. And in all this the man saw no agency except what lay outside himself, for which reason, and because of his ingenuity *the villagers called him the American*." See also Ronald Segal, *The Americans,* chapter 5, "The Unhappy Americans."

50. Arthur M. Schlesinger, Jr., *The Politics of Upheaval; The Age of Roosevelt,* Vol. III (Cambridge, Mass.: Riverside Press, 1960).
51. See René Cumont and Bernard Roiser, *The Hungry Future,* trans. Rosamund Linnell and R. B. Sutcliff (New York: Praeger, 1969).
52. See Richard Harris, *Justice* (Philadelphia: J. B. Lippincott Co., 1970), for a factual comparison between the administrations of Ramsey Clark and John Mitchell as Attorneys General.

53. Reich, *The Greening of America*, p. 4.
54. Michael Harrington's famous quote; see Israel Shenker, "Tract Record," *The New York Times Book Review*, January 24, 1971.
55. See Richard Lemon, *The Troubled American* (New York: Simon & Schuster, 1970), and Richard M. Scammon and Ben J. Wattenberg, *The Real Majority* (New York: Coward-McCann, 1970).
56. See Gary Wills, *Nixon Agonistes: The Crisis of the Self-Made Man* (Boston: Houghton Mifflin Co., 1970). This valuable study is more than a biography of Mr. Nixon, although it probes both the man and his policies. It encompasses "an image of some of the emotional, ideological, technological, and even environmental forces that play upon the American voter and make him choose the kind of public spokesmen . . . who occupy the White House."
57. See Langdon Gilkey, *How the Church Can Minister to the World Without Losing Itself*, pp. 31-33.
58. Commager, *The American Mind*, p. 456.
59. Series, "Are We in the Middle of the Second American Revolution?" *New York Times Magazine*, May, 1970.
60. Winter, *Being Free*, p. 140.

4. Dissent in America

1. Quoted in Oscar and Mary F. Handlin, *Commonwealth, A Study of the Role of Government in American Economy: Massachusetts, 1774-1861* (New York: New York University Press, 1947), p. 5.
2. Arthur M. Schlesinger, Jr., "Reinhold Niebuhr's Role in American Political Thought and Life," in Charles W. Kegley and Robert W. Bretall, ed., *Reinhold Niebuhr, His Religious, Social, and Political Thought* (New York: The Macmillan Co., 1961), p. 126.
3. Quoted, *ibid.*, pp. 128-29. See also Gabriel Fackre, *The Promise of Reinhold Niebuhr* (Philadelphia: J. B. Lippincott Co., 1970).
4. See Richard Neuhaus' section in Peter Berger and Richard Neuhaus, *Movement and Revolution* (New York: Harper & Row, 1970).
5. Political activists in the seats of power—McGovern, Hatfield, Muskie, Goodell, Gore, Fulbright, Javits—have been checked in Washington or defeated at the polls.
6. See Barry Goldwater, *The Conscience of a Majority* (Englewood Cliffs, N. J.: Prentice-Hall, 1970). Senator Goldwater is convinced that the conservative trend in national politics is growing. The mid-term elections, 1970, did not support his argument.
7. Hofstadter and Wallace, *American Violence*, pp. 475 ff.
8. See Vernon L. Parrington, *Main Currents in American Thought* (New

York: Harcourt, Brace, and Company, 1927-30), Vol. I. See also Hofstadter and Wallace, *American Violence*, pp. 47, 48, 52, 63, 66, 72, 76, 109, 110, 112, 115, 187, 270, 295, and 445.

9. Hendrick, *Lincoln's War Cabinet*. The courts overruled President Lincoln's high-handed (dictatorial) act.

10. See Jacques Ellul, *Violence* (New York: Seabury Press, 1969) for a significant contemporary Christian statement on the nature of violent dissent.

11. Whereas Jefferson, a hundred years later, argued against established religion because he did not want clerics meddling in civil affairs, Williams had argued earlier against the Constantine charter because he did not want civil authorities to have a voice over any man's conscience. See Martin E. Marty, *Righteous Empire*, pp. 35-45, on civil and religious settlement. See also James H. Smylie, "Protestant Clergy, the First Amendment and Beginnings of a Constitutional Debate," in Elwyn A. Smith, ed., *The Religion of the Republic*, pp. 116-53.

12. Samuel Eliot Morison and Henry Steele Commager, *The Growth of the American Republic, 1865-1942* (New York: Oxford University Press, 1942), p. 231.

13. Merle Curti, Richard H. Shryock, Thomas C. Cochran, and Fred Harvey Harrington, *An American History*, I (New York: Harper & Row, 1950), 85.

14. Edwin Scott Gaustad, ed., *Religious Issues in American History* (New York: Harper & Row, 1968), pp. 28-63.

15. *Ibid.*, p. 206.

16. The acts were passed by the Federalists in their attacks on dissenting Republican legislators and editors. Their effort to curb free speech and dissent boomeranged; they lost the next national election.

17. Hofstadter *et al.*, *The United States*, pp. 178-79.

18. Quoted in Hofstadter and Wallace, *American Violence*, pp. 475-76.

19. *Ibid.*, p. 11.

20. Ray Allen Billington, *The Protestant Crusade* (New York: The Macmillan Co., 1938), p. 387. See also Charles H. Sanderson, *White Protestant Americans, From National Origins to Religious Groups* (Englewood Cliffs, N. J.: Prentice-Hall, 1970), pp. 97-103.

21. *White Protestant Americans*, p. 15.

22. Michaelsen, *Piety in the Public School* (New York: The Macmillan Co., 1970), p. 45.

23. Morison and Commager, *The Growth of the American Republic, 1865-1942*, p. 155.

24. See Marty, *Righteous Empire*, pp. 203-9.

25. Hofstadter and Wallace, *American Violence*, pp. 133-79.

NOTES

26. Quoted in Schlesinger, *The Politics of Upheaval,* p. 600.
27. Galbraith, *The Affluent Society* (New York: The Macmillan Co., 1959), and *The New Industrial State* (The Macmillan Co., 1961).
28. Morison and Commager, *The Growth of the American Republic, 1865-1942,* p. 261.
29. *Ibid.,* p. 259.
30. *Ibid.,* p. 263.
31. See Hofstadter and Wallace, *American Violence.* The documents on violence from colonial days to the present are collected and classified: Political Violence, Economic Violence, Racial Violence, Religious and Ethnic Violence, Police Violence, Political Murders.
32. See Elmer T. Clark, *The Small Sects in America* (Nashville: Abingdon Press, 1954).
33. Schlissel, *Conscience in America* (New York: E. P. Dutton & Co., 1968), p. 18.
34. *Ibid.,* p. 19.
35. *Ibid.*
36. Quoted *ibid.,* p. 94.
37. Quoted *ibid.* p. 420.
38. See Telford Taylor, *Nuremberg and Vietnam: An American Tragedy* (New York: New York Times Publishing Co., 1970). Brigadier General Taylor, chief United States prosecutor at Nuremberg, is presently professor of law at Columbia University. In any war the notion that the victor can be an impartial judge violates the canons of jurisprudence and ignores the realities of human nature.
39. Mulford Q. Sibley, ed., *The Quiet Battle, Writings on the Theory and Practice of Non-Violent Resistance* (Boston: Beacon Press, 1963), p. 305.
40. *Ibid.,* pp. 305-6.
41. Albert Bigelow, *The Voyage of the Golden Rule: An Experiment with Truth* (Garden City, N. Y.: Doubleday & Co., 1959). But "civil disobedience" is only possible in a rule of law and order such as is found in the more mature democracies.
42. *Ibid.,* p. 143, quoted in Sibley, *The Quiet Battle,* p. 306.
43. Neil Haworth's moving account, "Civil Disobedience at Newport News," is included in Sibley, *The Quiet Battle,* pp. 308-12.
44. Quoted *ibid.,* p. 307.
45. Quoted in James Finn, *A Conflict of Loyalties* (New York: Pegasus, 1968), p. 8. The "religious" qualification was expanded in 1970.
46. *Ibid.*
47. Mulford Q. Sibley, *The Obligation to Disobey, Conscience and the Law* (New York: Council of Religion and International Affairs, 1970), pp. 7-8.

48. Sibley, "Dissent and Law," p. 360. I am indebted to Professor Sibley's essay on "The Relevance of Non-Violence in Our Day" for this four-point summary statement (*The Quiet Battle*, pp. 357-77). I am also indebted to his *The Obligation to Disobey*.

49. *Foreign Policy*, Fall, 1970. See also Andrew J. Pierre, "Nuclear Diplomacy: Britain, France, and America," *Foreign Affairs*, XLIX (1971) 283-301.

50. "Plain Lessons of a Bad Decade," *Foreign Policy*, Fall, 1970.

51. "Cool It: The Foreign Policy of Young America," *ibid.*

52. During 1970, in Illinois, 2,000 young people—many who were *not* in college—called up for induction refused to serve, and went to court.

53. These two cases and Judge Doyle's observations are based on an unpublished address by Paul A. Mueller, Jr., Esq., to the Franklin and Marshall College Lancaster County Alumni Society, November, 1970.

54. Lancaster *Intelligencer-Journal*, December 29, 1970. That decision was reversed by a higher court in mid-March, 1971.

55. Reuben A. Sheares, II, "Beyond White Theology," *Christianity and Crisis*, XXX (1970) 229.

56. *Ibid.*

57. *Ibid.*

58. Foreword to William H. Grier and Price M. Cobbs, *Black Rage* (New York: Bantam Books, 1968), pp. 7-8.

59. Vivian, *Black Power and the American Myth* (Philadelphia: Fortress Press, 1970), p. 3.

60. *The New York Times'* descriptive citation on *Black Rage*.

61. Grier and Cobbs, *Black Rage*, p. 2.

62. *Report of the National Advisory Commission on Civil Disorders.*

63. Andrew N. Greeley, "Turning Off the People," *The New Republic*, June 27, 1970, p. 15.

64. See Arthur Simon, "A Stroke of the Pen," *Commonweal*, January 22, 1971, pp. 391-95, in which he calls for an executive order from the President to open towns and suburbs to black and lower income families. (The order could be given under Title VI of the 1964 Civil Rights Bill.)

65. "Personal Glimpses," *The Reader's Digest*, December, 1970, p. 127.

66. Page Smith, *Daughters of the Promised Land* (Boston: Little, Brown and Co., 1970), pp. 103-4.

67. *Ibid.*, p. 120.

68. *Ibid.*

69. Quoted in Smith, *Daughters of the Promised Land*, p. 121.

70. *Catholic World*, January, 1971, pp. 177-83.

5. The Church and the State

1. I am indebted for this delineation to H. Richard Niebuhr, *Christ and Culture* (New York: Harper & Row, 1951). Dr. Niebuhr acknowledges his debt to the pioneering work of Adolf Harnack.
2. Stewart Herman's *It's Your Souls We Want* (New York: Harper & Row, 1941), a study of the Nazi State, is as insightful today as when it was first published.
3. *The Christian Century*, October 2, 1968, p. 1233.
4. See Kyle Haselden, *The Racial Problem in Christian Perspective* (Nashville: Broadman Press, 1964).
5. Hacker, *The End of the American Era*. The other side of the coin is that many laymen resent the claims of the gospel on their *private* lives—worship, evangelism, stewardship, meaningful family relationships. Lord Melbourne, leaving an evangelistic service, exploded angrily, "Things have come to a pretty pass when religion is made to invade the sphere of *private* life." The writer has experienced more travail in proclaiming the gospel concretely on "private" issues than on "public" issues. "Privatism" is strong in the American character.
6. See Seward Hiltner, *Self-Understanding* (Nashville: Abingdon Press, 1962), chapter 4, for a lucid discussion of "dated emotions." They plague not only individuals but groups in society.
7. See Robert M. Grant, *Augustus to Constantine: The Thrust of the Christian Movement into the Roman World* (New York: Harper & Row, 1970), p. 43.
8. Will Herberg, *Protestant, Catholic, Jew,* and Martin Marty, *The New Shape of American Religion* (New York: Harper & Row, 1959); see also, Fisher, *From Tradition to Mission*, chapters 1-3, for an examination of this in a particular church and city in Pennsylvania.
9. "On Political Authority," *The Works of Martin Luther*, Vol. III (Philadelphia: Fortress Press, 1957).
10. See Reinhold Niebuhr, *Moral Man and Immoral Society* (New York: Charles Scribner's Sons, 1932).
11. Bennett, *Christians and the State*, chapters 5-8.
12. Commager, *The American Mind*, p. 163. See also Robert N. Bellah, "Civil Religion in America."
13. H. Richard Niebuhr, *The Meaning of Revelation* (New York: The Macmillan Co., 1941), p. 182.
14. Norman Gall, "Latin America: The Church Militant," *Commentary*, April, 1970, pp. 26-28.
15. See chapters 3 and 4. See also Mead, *The Lively Experiment*, chapters 4-7.

16. See Fisher, *Preface to Parish Renewal,* chapter 2, for a presentation to laymen on discerning the Word of God in the words of men.
17. Gilkey, *How the Church Can Minister to the World Without Losing Itself,* pp. 60-61.
18. Archibald M. Hunter, *The Message of the New Testament* (Philadelphia: Westminster Press, 1944), pp. 53-62, provides a scholarly presentation in laymen's language.
19. Grant, *Augustus to Constantine,* chapters 4, 10, 19, and 21.
20. Quoted in *Christianity and Crisis,* April 27, 1964.
21. See Herberg, *Protestant, Catholic, Jew.*
22. Grant, *Augustus to Constantine,* is a thorough study on how this occurred in Christianity's first three hundred years.
23. Bennett, *Christians and the State,* p. 278.
24. See Grant, *Augustus to Constantine,* pp. 3-45 and 77-78.
25. Cullmann, *The State in the New Testament,* pp. 71-85.
26. Bennett, *Christians and the State,* p. 36.
27. Essentially this is Aristotle's view of the state. See chapter 2, "The American Democratic State," part I.
28. Quoted in Bennett, *Christians and the State,* p. 37.
29. "On Political Authority," *The Works of Martin Luther,* III, 258.
30. Bennett, *Christians and the State,* p. 59.
31. Quoted *ibid.,* pp. 41-42. My summary statement on the views of Augustine, Luther, and Calvin is based partially on chapters 3-5 in Bennett's study. For a more exhaustive inquiry see John Bowle, *Western Political Thought, An Historical Introduction from the Origins to Rousseau* (London: Jonathan Cape, 1947), pp. 124-44, 270-87.
32. Timothy L. Smith, *Revivalism and Social Reform in Mid-Nineteenth Century America* (Nashville: Abingdon Press, 1957), p. 35.
33. Bennett, *Christians and the State,* p. 57. One also recalls Lord Acton's judgment: "Power tends to corrupt and absolute power corrupts absolutely."
34. *Ibid.,* p. 278.
35. Herman Will, Jr., "How Churches Influence National Policy," *Christian Advocate,* December 24, 1970.
36. Bennett, *Christians and the State,* p. 279.
37. Nichols, *Religion and American Democracy,* p. 50.
38. *Ibid.,* p. 57.
39. *Ibid.,* p. 58. Arminianism holds that man contributes to his own salvation. It centers on human rather than divine activity as a reaction to extreme Calvinist predestination. See Willston Walker, *A History of the Christian Church* (New York: Charles Scribner's Sons, 1959) pp. 399 ff.
40. *Religion and American Democracy,* p. 58.

41. *Ibid.*, p. 59.
42. *Ibid.*, p. 85.
43. *Ibid.*, p. 91.
44. *Ibid.*
45. *Ibid.*
46. Bennett, *Christians and the State*, p. 280.

6. Political Integrity in the American Church

1. Mead, *The Lively Experiment*, p. 68.
2. Robert Michaelson, *Piety in the Public School*, p. 45. This is an excellent work which enables one to understand why most Americans view public education as a "sacred" American institution.
3. Matthew 22:21.
4. Adams, *The Growing Church Lobby in Washington*, pp. 11 ff. Mr. Adams also notes: "The new-breed church lobbyist likes the feel of power as much as the old-line politician. It's apparently a universal urge to which churchmen are not immune. Albert Saunders, young secretary for national affairs of the United Presbyterian Church, U.S.A., bluntly informed me: 'suddenly we in the field of religious social action found ourselves playing the role of political power groups—and many of us liked it.' Saunders was referring to the sustained effort of church activists who joined with liberal labor and civil rights organizations to lobby for the passage of the Civil Rights Act of 1964. The merging of labor, church, and civil rights forces for one common goal produced the short-lived coalition of conscience and power of the Kennedy-Johnson administrations. The role of the church in the bill's passage was a key one, and church lobbyists, for weal or woe, have never been the same. The involvement of church activists in the thorny issues of the 1960's—the decade of great social change—gave the church a new political dimension."
5. See Thomas C. Oden, *Beyond Revolution; A Response to the Underground Church* (Philadelphia: Westminster Press, 1970). The author is not speaking of liberals like Berrigans, Groppe, *et al.*, who "do their thing" without insisting arrogantly that their way is the only way.
6. Campbell and Holloway, *Up to Our Steeples in Politics*.
7. Herman Will, Jr., "How Churches Influence National Policy," p. 9.
8. Quoted in Jorstad, *The Politics of Doomsday*, p. 68.
9. Will, "How Churches Influence National Policy."
10. See Fisher, *From Tradition to Mission* and *The Affable Enemy* for descriptions of and prescriptions for conversion of this ecclesiastical disposition.

11. See Richard Neuhaus, "American Ethos and the Revolutionary Option," *World View*, December, 1970, pp. 5-9, especially p. 6.
12. Jürgen Moltmann, "Politics and the Practice of Hope," *The Christian Century*, March 11, 1970, pp. 288-301.
13. See Fisher, *From Tradition to Mission*, chapter 3, "Confrontation and Response," describing the results of political integrity in a particular church.
14. Bridston, *Church Politics* (New York: The World Publishing Company, 1969), pp. 10-11.
15. *Ibid.*, p. 164.
16. *Ibid.*, p. 148.
17. *Ibid.*, pp. 146-47. Professor Bridston argues cogently that "whatever public discussion positively contributes to the health of the body politic in terms of building up the *esprit de corps* by the feeling of general participation, the lack of discussion in the ecclesiastical ballot system has a definite, negative limitation as a democratic voting procedure. . . . Furthermore, the ecclesiastical ballot (and its related forms of voting) facilitates the control of a large organization by a small in-group. The political "ins" not only have greater public exposure throughout the membership but they also, by virtue of the offices they hold, are more often in touch with one another and therefore more able to mobilize themselves and to organize their political power in the interests of their concerns or candidates. The deceptive element in all this is, of course, that such "ecclesiastical" political devices as the Roman ballot *appear* to be nonpolitical, particularly to the uninitiated 'outsiders.' This is especially true in church conventions in which a 'nonpolitical' atmosphere is assiduously cultivated. For the ecclesiastical 'team' therefore, the playing of 'discrepant roles' has been made easier than for most political groups by presumed nonpolitical character of their activities as well as by the fact, already mentioned, that the church politician wields unusual power through the magical transference from sacramental to political authority projected on the priest-pastor."
18. Other causes have been identified and addressed by critical evaluators: Peter Berger, *The Noise of Solemn Assemblies* (New York: Harper & Row, 1961); Gibson Winter, *The Suburban Captivity of the Church* (Harper & Row, 1962); Robert Raines, *New Life in the Church* (Harper & Row, 1963); Wallace E. Fisher, *From Tradition to Mission, Preface to Parish Renewal, The Affable Enemy,* and *Can Man Hope to be Human?*
19. Bridston, *Church Politics,* p. 163. See also Stephen Rose, *Who's Killing the Church?* (New York: Harper & Row, 1968); and James Gustafson, *Treasure in Earthen Vessels* (Harper & Row, 1961), chapter 3, "The Church: a Political Community."

20. Paul Ramsey, *Who Speaks for the Church?* The report of the Geneva Conference is also in print: *Christians in the Technical and Social Revolutions of Our Time: World Conference on Church and Society: Official Report* (Geneva: World Council of Churches, 1967).

21. *Who Speaks For the Church?* p. 170.

22. *Ibid.,* p. 27.

23. *Ibid.,* p. 55.

24. *Ibid.*

25. *Ibid.,* p. 152.

26. *Ibid.*

27. *Ibid.,* p. 149.

28. *Ibid.,* p. 156.

29. See O. Fred Nolde, *The Churches and the Nations* (Philadelphia: Fortress Press, 1970); James Finn, ed., *A Conflict of Loyalties;* and William O. Douglas, *Points of Rebellion* (New York: Vintage Books, 1970).

30. See Ramsey, *Who Speaks for the Church?* pp. 47-52, for an exchange of opinion with Ralph Potter of Harvard Divinity School on this point.

31. Thielicke, *Theological Ethics,* II, 68.

32. John W. Gardner, *No Easy Victories* (New York: Harper & Row, 1968), p. 43.

33. Adams, *The Growing Church Lobby in Washington.*

34. Mr. Taft, the uncle of Senator Robert Taft, Jr., has served as the mayor of Cincinnati. A responsible member of Christ Episcopal Church in that city, Mr. Taft has also served as a president of the National Council of Churches.

35. Will, "How Churches Influence National Policy," pp. 9-10.

36. We are speaking here of the National Association of Evangelicals (NAE) with whom main-line Protestantism can and should cooperate. We shall speak of the ultra-fundamentalists below.

37. Adams, *The Growing Church Lobby in Washington,* p. 139.

38. *Ibid.,* p. 139. The italics are mine. See also Erling Jorstad, "Two on the Right: A Comparative Look at Fundamentalism and New Evangelicalism," *The Lutheran Quarterly,* (1971), 107-17.

39. I have relied on Richard Hofstadter, *The Paranoid Style in American Politics* (New York: Vintage Books, 1967) and *Anti-Intellectualism in American Life* (New York: Alfred A. Knopf, 1963); Winthrop S. Hudson, *Religion in America* (New York: Charles Scribner's Sons, 1965); Erling Jorstad, *The Politics of Doomsday;* Ralph Lord Roy, *Apostles of Discord* (Boston: Beacon Press, 1953) and *Your Church——Their Target* (Arlington, Va.: Better Books, 1966); Harry and Bonaro Overstreet, *The Strange Tactics of Extremism* (New York: W. W.

Norton and Co., 1964). Dr. Jorstad, professor of history at St. Olaf College, provides the most thorough specific study.

40. Jorstad, *The Politics of Doomsday*, p. 14.
41. *Ibid.*, pp. 19-37; also Hofstadter, *The Paranoid Style in American Politics*, pp. 41-92. Dr. Hofstadter is the late professor of American history at Columbia University.
42. Jorstad, *The Politics of Doomsday*, p. 41.
43. Hofstadter, *The Paranoid Style in American Politics*, pp. 3-41. Hofstadter points out that he is not using the term "paranoid" in the clinical sense. "When I speak of the paranoid style, I use the term much as a historian of art might speak of the Baroque or the Mannerist style. . . . In the paranoid style, as I conceive it, the feeling of persecution is central, and it is indeed systematized in grandiose theories of conspiracy. . . . The spokesman of the paranoid style finds it directed against a nation, a culture, a way of life, whose fate affects not himself alone but millions of others. . . . His sense that his political passions are unselfish and patriotic, in fact, goes far to intensify his feeling of righteousness and his moral indignation" (p. 4).
44. *Ibid.*, pp. 133 ff. Hofstadter observed further: "While expansion was won so cheaply, the United States, thanks largely to its continental position, was enjoying, as C. Vann Woodward has pointed out, virtually free security—which, he suggests, should be given a place among the great shaping forces of our history alongside the free land of our continental interior. . . . Free security, easy expansion, inexpensive victories, decisive triumphs—such was almost our whole experience with the rest of the world down to the twentieth century. . . . It was only after the major effort of the Second World War, when we found ourselves not presiding over a pacified and docile world, but engaged in a worldwide stalemate and a costly and indecisive struggle in Korea, that the American people first experienced the full reality of what all the other great nations have long known—the situation of limited power. The illusion of American omnipotence remained, but the reality of American preponderance was gone. It is this shock to the American consciousness to which Goldwater and others appealed when they cried: "Why not victory?" Why not, indeed, when one remembers all those facile triumphs? In this light it becomes possible to understand how Goldwater thought he could promise unremitting victories in the cold war along with balanced budgets and lower taxes. . . . And when one ponders how much the world position of America has changed within the past fifty years, what seems most remarkable is not that many should respond wholeheartedly to the pseudo-conservative interpretation of events, but that our statesmanship has been as restrained as it has usually been and that this restraint has won preponderant public support."

NOTES

45. See Jorstad, *The Politics of Doomsday*, chapter 7, "An Alliance for Action."
46. *Ibid.*, p. 154.
47. *Ibid.*
48. *The Philadelphia Inquirer*, January 16, 1971.
49. *Ibid.*
50. Quoted in Jorstad, *The Politics of Doomsday*, p. 158.
51. *Ibid.* To call this particular denominational periodical "liberal" in the context of other leading "liberal" journals—Protestant and Catholic— is a gross exaggeration.
52. *Ibid.*, p. 53.
53. *Ibid.*, p. 54.
54. Quoted *ibid.*, pp. 81-2. See also Theodore Sorenson, *Kennedy* (New York: Harper & Row, 1965), pp. 334-36.
55. *The Politics of Doomsday*, p. 100.
56. Hofstadter, *The Paranoid Style in American Politics*, p. 137. The italics are mine.